MECHANICS OF INNOVATION

INVENT · PROTECT · FUND · DIRECT

THE ESSENTIAL HANDBOOK
FOR
INVENTORS, ENGINEERS,
SCIENTISTS, & PHYSICIANS

RICHARD J. MCMURTREY

Mechanics of Innovation
The Essential Handbook for Inventors, Engineers, Scientists, & Physicians
Invent – Protect – Fund – Direct
Richard J. McMurtrey

All quotations herein are verified and are used with permission or in the public domain. In particular, I express tremendous gratitude to the Albert Einstein Archives at the Hebrew University of Jerusalem for their assistance and permission.

Library of Congress Catalog Control Data

McMurtrey, Richard J.
    Mechanics of innovation; the essential handbook for inventors, engineers, scientists,
    & physicians / Richard J. McMurtrey
        p. cm.
Includes index
ISBN-10: 0985396318
ISBN-13: 978-0-9853963-1-2
Library of Congress Control Number: 2012943207

ACKNOWLEDGMENTS

I would like to thank my friends, colleagues, and mentors who have helped me along the way and made this path possible, particularly:

Zhiyi Zuo, M.D., Ph.D.----- University of Virginia Medical Center, Departments of Anesthesiology, Neuroscience, & Neurological Surgery

Ulli Bayer, Ph.D.------------- University of Colorado Health Sciences Center, Department of Pharmacology

Tate Tischner, J.D.----------- LeClairRyan Law Firm

Ryan S. McMurtrey--------- United States Marine Corps

Jenny Redford, D.D.S.------ United States Air Force

Amy K. Guzik, M.D.-------- University of California San Diego, Department of Neurosciences

Carl E. Patton, Ph.D.-------- Colorado State University, Department of Physics

John M. Knab, M.B.A.------ Inventor/Innovator

Benjamin D. Hoehn, M.D., Ph.D.---- GenomicTree

Scott C. Steffensen, Ph.D.-------------- Brigham Young University, Neuroscience Center

Michael A. Keene, Ph.D., M.B.A.---- Westminster College, Technology Management Program

TABLE OF CONTENTS

LIST OF TABLES

§

INTRODUCTION

"I wished to live deliberately,
to front only the essential facts of life,
and see if I could not learn what it had to teach,
and not, when I came to die, discover that I had not lived....
I wanted to live deep and suck out all the marrow of life."
Henry David Thoreau, *Walden*

"Two roads diverged in a wood, and I—
I took the one less traveled by,
And that has made all the difference."
Robert Frost, *The Road Not Taken*

When reading about the lives of many great thinkers and innovators throughout history, one cannot help but marvel at their ability to dedicate themselves to their work even when they were unsure whether their efforts would be fruitful or not. By persevering, many were able to make great discoveries and contributions to the world, even when no one else believed in them. Such is the process of innovation, often a lonely and less-traveled road. But by following in the footsteps of great minds who have gone before, new innovators can challenge current frames of thinking and show that there is still much more to learn and discover, and by hard work and perseverance they too can contribute something meaningful to humanity.

Many people recognize unmet needs in their daily work and conceive of novel solutions to these problems. This takes a certain mindset, of course, one of curiosity and inquiry. There are many instances where insightful individuals conceive of solutions and ideas before others have even acknowledged that there is a problem or need for improvement. But in this age of technology and in today's competitive atmosphere, innovation alone is not enough—one must also understand logistics, legalities, patents, finance, grants, private equity, regulatory compliance, market strategy, and many other aspects in order to advance new ideas and bring meaningful technologies into use. The world has increasing need for cross-disciplinary specialists who can integrate fields and span barriers, particularly the chasms between business, science, and technology.

This book creates a framework for building innovation from the elements of ideas. It describes specific steps of how to create a company, obtain funding, invent and protect ideas, manage a company, commercialize technology, and much more. In addition, this book includes several outlines for detailed business plans, operating agreements, investor presentations, SBIR/STTR grant applications, and research studies, as well as other useful appendices and resources, which will be of great benefit to any entrepreneur. With this knowledge, any innovator or inventor can establish, fund, and grow a startup company from the ground up. Creating something meaningful out of a mere idea has been the magic and inspiration of many great and successful entrepreneurs of our time.

This handbook evolved out of learning experiences and a compilation of notes over time, and as with all learning, should be considered a work in progress. It aims to cover the practical tasks of establishing and growing a company, whether in medicine, engineering, science, or any other endeavor. This book will also serve as a valuable resource for universities and institutions, helping professors, researchers, and students catalyze new innovations. Many universities are realizing that it is mutually beneficial to support spin-off companies from their technologies, both for the prestige and the financial rewards.

Many researchers stumble onto great technologies and ideas, and although many researchers are naturally more interested in the technology than the business of the technology, creating a business is often the only way to ever bring the technology to the public. Surprisingly, the technical skills to accomplish this are entirely neglected in the curriculum of most graduate and professional degree programs, and the translational research gap perpetuates. This book serves as an essential guide, covering gaps in business, legal, and regulatory education for those seeking to create their own companies around their ideas.

The *National Institutes of Health* (NIH) has recognized this translational training gap in M.D. and Ph.D. programs, for example, and recently formed the *National Center for Translational Sciences* (NCATS) to help educate and fund the translation of new science into meaningful technologies and products. The FDA also recognizes the need to better educate scientists and entrepreneurs on how to navigate the chaos of funding and fulfilling regulatory hurdles.

Without a company behind an idea, technologies cannot be appropriately developed and commercialized, and thus the innovation is lost. Academic institutions rarely have the resources or abilities to develop a technology beyond a prototype stage. University technologies must typically be licensed to and developed by companies, and sometimes these companies are created by the same university professors who created the technology. Understanding how technology is developed and brought to market is therefore essential information for all professionals.

Research is the fundamental driver of technology. Yet over time even some large companies have trended towards minimization of R&D workforce and budgets. This stems from multiple factors, including the intrinsic risks of new ideas, costs and expertise requirements, lack of foresight in expanding innovation, or the fact that minimizing expenses maximizes short-term profits, but this all clearly comes at the expense of the innovation of tomorrow. Once a product is successfully on the market, it is easy to reap the rewards and neglect putting a percentage of those profits back into new innovations and advancements. Hence companies rise and fall as technology develops. But the great advantage is that this creates large windows of opportunity for new innovations to arise through independent startup companies.

Another advantage of small startup companies is the passion and excitement of the founders. They have not lost sight of their ideas and dreams, and they believe in what they have to offer. They are not necessarily concerned with pleasing shareholders or with big profits—they simply want to contribute something meaningful to the world. Interestingly, large companies are increasingly looking for small innovative companies to acquire in order to feed their new product pipeline. This creates ideal opportunities for new innovators and entrepreneurs who, though lacking the resources of a large company, make up for it with their passion, vision, and creativity.

Thus this book is written not just for companies with solid financial resources, but for small companies and startups that may operate on a minimal budget or that may even begin as only a "virtual company" or "micro-corporation." It therefore discusses many hints of how to build a successful company on a minimal budget (e.g., using non-dilutive grant funding and minimizing operating costs and burn rates), particularly in early stages when many innovators may rely on their own personal funds to create their ideas.

Those willing to venture into the chaotic and intriguing world of entrepreneurship should find this information invaluable. The resources included here may also stimulate new ideas and paths for technologies and funding resources. Along the journey, you will likely make many great friends and colleagues, and you may also face skepticism from those who have far more resources or opposition from those who follow lines of rote sciolism, but try to use every experience and challenge as a learning opportunity and do not be discouraged. In the words of Alfred Lord Tennyson, from his poem *Ulysses*:

> *Yet all experience is an arch wherethro'*
> *Gleams that untraveled world whose margin fades*
> *For ever and for ever when I move.*

§

PART I – STARTUP LOGISTICS

"We should come home from far,
from adventures, and perils, and discoveries every day,
with new experience and character."
Henry David Thoreau, *Walden*

"Experience is the name everyone gives to their mistakes."
Oscar Wilde, *Lady Windermere's Fan*

Creating innovation demands a unique set of talents and characteristics: it requires the seed of a great idea, plus innovative vision, brilliant problem-solving, practical thinking, and unbreakable perseverance. Many innovators derived new ideas and created technologies that were at first unimagined or misunderstood. Taking an idea from conceptualization to completion can seem daunting, but the challenge can be exciting and rewarding.

Many ideas begin as a side project, simultaneously fueling and consuming one's energy. While altogether enthralling and daunting, building one's own "creation" is a very fulfilling endeavor. There may never be an ideal time in life to take these sorts of risks, but even if an idea fails, the lessons learned can be essential to achieving success with the next idea. For a variety of reasons (discussed throughout), many ideas and technologies must be built within the framework and legal protections of a company.

Business Registration

To establish a legal business entity, business registration is done with the state, and the business will be subject to that state's business laws and regulations.

Most states have an online business registration system that makes the process quite simple — see Appendix I for state business registration websites. You will also need to obtain an *Employer Identification Number* (EIN), which registers the business with the federal government. The EIN is basically like a Social Security Number for the business, and will be used on many financial documents, bank accounts, taxes, grants, and business licensing. The EIN registration can be obtained by filling out form SS-4 or, more conveniently, by visiting the IRS.gov website — it takes about 5-10 minutes: https://sa1.www4.irs.gov/modiein/individual/index.jsp.

At this time you will choose the legal structure of the business. For many early stage start-up tech companies, the easiest and most convenient choice is a *Limited Liability Company* (LLC). This creates a company that is its own legal entity and appropriately shields many legal liabilities. Even though an LLC is essentially the equivalent of a corporation, it is not the same thing. A *corporation* (technically, a C-corporation) is the most traditional business organization. An LLC is a company structure that actually offers much more flexibility and ease of operation than a corporation. Both business structures provide nearly identical legal protections, but a corporation generally has more administrative burdens and different tax rules.

Both an LLC and a corporation typically require standard paperwork to be filed when registering with the state: a corporation files *Articles of Incorporation*, whereas an LLC files *Articles of Organization*, which is often joined with some form of an *Operating Agreement* or *Bylaws*. These documents list the company's legal name, the operating location or main office, and any and all owners, shareholders, board members, and/or officers. They also can lay out general policies of the business such as authority assurance, voting rights, meeting schedules, total number of shares in the company, rules for common/preferred stock, rules for transfer of stock, as well as rights and obligations of the owners/shareholders. A simplified example of this is provided in Appendix II.

Many other forms of Articles of Organization and Operating Agreements can also be found online for little to no cost, and an attorney can help tailor agreements that best protect the company and all parties involved (this is particularly important for multi-owner entities or any unique or complex circumstances). All business documents should be written for your specific needs and circumstances.

Businesses can also file additional policies, agreements, bylaws, shareholder agreements, or other legal documents with the state at a later time if they choose. Minimizing the number of founders is advantageous in that it minimizes the potential for disagreements or conflict; even amongst friends, there should be a clear understanding of who makes the final decisions, how much time is expected, who owns assets, who is responsible for financing, and other general company policies.

Company Structure

Regarding the differences between a corporation and an LLC, a corporation has more administrative layers than an LLC: in a corporation, a board of directors is first organized and then appoints executive officers and a registered agent for the corporation. In some states these positions can all be held by the same person, although clearly the corporation is designed to provide certain distinct powers to directors, officers, and shareholders. A corporation also has certain administrative tasks to adhere to, such as additional tax forms, annual reports, annual election of directors, meetings of directors and shareholders, and record keeping of board decisions and meeting minutes. Corporations tend to operate on their own fiscal year, whereas an LLC usually accounts on a calendar year.

The founders of a corporation are typically appointed as chief executives, whereas the owners of an LLC are typically called chief members or principle members, but other titles such as president, owner, or founder are also used. In fact, an LLC can even choose to designate a board of directors and have executive officers like a corporation. There are, however, important differences between an LLC and a corporation in the rules for company shares and stock ownership.

In a corporation, the amount of capital invested in the company usually must correspond directly to a fair valuation of share ownership. As an example, if a founder invests $4,000 and a second investor provides $6,000, they should own 40% and 60% respectively. This may actually be based on several other factors, such as other legal agreements and company valuation (discussed later), but suffice it to say that for a corporation, the separation of capital contribution and ownership share can be a complicated issue, requiring various legal agreements and tax considerations.

An LLC, on the other hand, provides a clearer means for keeping capital contributions separate from ownership shares, allowing assignment of ownership separately from capital contributed. So in the example above, each person could agree to own 50% of the company despite their differing contributions.

An LLC also has a *pass-through* or *disregard* tax status, which automatically passes profits through the company to its owners, thus avoiding the double taxation on both the company's profits and the owner's profits. The pass-through status allows the company's tax filings to be submitted with the owner's tax filings, i.e., the standard LLC allows tax reporting of company earnings to be reported to the IRS in the same paperwork as the owner's personal tax filings if the owner so chooses. Alternatively, an LLC can choose to file its own taxes independent of the owners. If desired, an LLC can even be converted into corporate status for tax purposes (by filing IRS form 8832), or even converted to an official C-corporation by re-registering with the state (often done when potential investors prefer this structure). However, a corporation cannot convert back to the pass-through or disregard LLC status once this is done. For certain reasons though, a corporation may elect pass-through status by filing IRS form 2553 to elect S-corporation status.

Both types of structures can choose to offer equity incentives to employees (e.g., employee stock options, restricted stock awards, etc.). Corporations can allow payments of stock options, stock awards, etc. with deferred taxation or minimized personal taxation under several conditions, whereas an LLC pass-through status means that equity, stock awards, dividends, or salary will typically need to be counted as personal earnings and subject to income and/or capital gains taxation in that same reporting period.

In all, corporations and LLCs can carry out essentially the same functions with their shares, but offering public shares is more complicated with LLCs, and equity compensation is more likely to carry individual tax-burdens in an LLC than in a corporation. On the other hand, separating capital investment from percentage of ownership is more complicated with corporations. Therefore, many companies use a strategy of starting with a simple LLC structure then converting to a corporation at the appropriate time, such as with the first major equity investment in the company or when offering initial public shares.

There are also other legal business structures which are not often used except in certain situations. A *Professional Limited Liability Company* (PLLC) can be used for service-oriented businesses, specifically for those that provide services of a licensed professional, such as medical, legal, or engineering services. A *General Partnership* is usually a partnership of two or more persons who agree to jointly invest time, money, property, or labor in exchange for certain pre-agreed terms of ownership or profit sharing. A *Limited Partnership* is used in cases where a general partner(s) manages the company and is responsible for all debts, and a limited partner(s) maintains a limited liability and simply provides investment or other resources for a share of the company and its profits. A *Limited Liability Partnership* (LLP) imparts limited liability to the above-mentioned Limited Partnership or General Partnership. *Sole Proprietorship* is a status for a self-employed, independently run venture with no investors, and usually only requires an EIN if you begin paying wages or for certain legal or tax reasons (such as filing certain tax reports, for grant funding, etc.).

Business Name

Registering your business involves registering a legal name for the business. Therefore, when choosing your company name, you should perform an internet search of your list of considerations to make sure no one has already used the name. This includes a search of domain names to see if anyone possesses the internet address you would use for your company (see *Internet Presence* below). With a little ingenuity, a unique word, perhaps even made-up, can capture attention and give subtle hints at your philosophy, character, and approach. A unique or made-up name is also more likely to be protectable by trademark. The legal name should include the business structure at the end—if you want to name your company *Technology*, as a generic example, the legal name of the company should be *Technology LLC* or *Technology, Inc.*, depending on what structure you choose. You can also register an assumed name, called the "Doing Business As" (DBA) name or the "Trade" name, such as *Technology* or *Tech* or *TCH* or whatever you would like the common name of your company to be, but it is usually easiest to keep the business name and

DBA name the same. The business and any DBA name will sometimes require registration with the local county or city in addition to the state registration.

Logistics & Setup

Most states will also ask you questions about your business to assess whether you will need to file tax reports annually or quarterly, and whether the nature of your business will require insurance, a sales tax license, or other registrations or compliances. If you do not yet have employees and are not yet selling anything, you will likely not need to file any of these things, because it will only add unnecessary paperwork and you can always update the status later. States may also want you to register your company with the state department of revenue or taxation for tax filing purposes, and should provide instructions on their business registration websites on how to do this.

Usually before selling a product you will need to obtain a sales license in the state and city/county where you are based. This is often offered at the time of the state business registration. Monthly, quarterly, or annual sales tax payments will be required, depending on the state. When purchasing items not for resale, you can usually avoid sales tax with an exemption, such as for R&D, manufacturing supplies, or equipment purchases (again depending on the state).

It is not unusual for a company to begin as a "virtual company" or "micro-corporation," which is essentially a legal organization of the company with a framework for protecting financial and intellectual property, without burning through money for facilities and administrative costs. This can be extraordinarily beneficial to a startup company if financing is limited, particularly during the early stage of organizing when technology is still in development, while securing IP protection, while administrative personnel are being assembled, or while funding is still being secured. In early startup the founders can often accomplish most administrative tasks via internet and home office, and needed lab space will depend on the technology being developed, and in some cases can be can be done in contracted research labs. If the work was originally conceived of or developed at a university, particularly if there is patent protection, the university will typically require a licensing

Item Price	Total
ntists, & $17.96	$17.96

	$17.96
	$17.96
it	$17.96
	$0.00

ng.

amazon.com

P

Your order of September 6, 2012 (Order ID 002-9444284-3480224

Qty.	Item
1	**Mechanics of Innovation: The Essential Handbook for Inventors, Engineers, S Physicians** McMurtrey, Richard J. --- Paperback **(** P-1-Q33D84 **) 0985396318**

Subtotal
Order Total
Paid via credit
Balance due

This shipment completes your order.

Have feedback on how we packaged your order? Tell us at www.amazon.com/pack

agreement before a spin-off company or business entity can commence work on the technology.

Internet Presence – Website Building

With the official establishment of a company, in most cases you will want to create an internet presence for the company. This will establish legitimacy for investors, grant reviewers, partners, and future collaborators. At minimum, a domain name should be registered for the company to prepare well for the future, as it often takes much time to gain a significant presence on the world wide web. Fortunately it has become quite easy to register a domain and build a website even if you have no experience or skill in web programming.

The first step is to find a hosting company, which is a company that charges a fee for providing your website and files to the online world. Each hosting company has a domain name search function to see if your proposed domain name (a.k.a. website address) is already taken, or you can check domain availability using www.whois.net. It typically costs around $10 to register a domain name (as an example, innovatorguide.com). It is easiest to purchase your domain name from your intended hosting company (rather than buying it from a random vendor and transferring it to your hosting company, since this would require updating the domain's DNS/nameservers).

The hosting company then charges an annual fee for the maintaining the function of your website. This is usually in the range of $100-$150 per year, depending on what services you use and how many domain names you run (typically the hosting company allows several domains to run at once for the same overall price). Hosting services also typically provide other options with your account, like integrated email and forwarding, secure database management, online shopping carts, etc. This is obviously much easier, cheaper, and safer than setting up your own hosting servers.

The host may also allow you to anonymously register the domain so that your contact information cannot be gathered from domain owner registries. It is best to pick a reliable and responsive hosting company, so look at all the accessory services, web building tools, bandwidth capabilities, and also read

11

reviews if possible. InMotion Hosting and Bluehost are two good options that provide all these services and options, but there are many others available.

For building or editing your website there are many options. The easiest is if the hosting company integrates a web building function into their services, allowing you to choose a template and edit text and images at your convenience. These web templates provide a great way to get a site up and running quickly and cheaply (note that it always takes a day after registering the domain before you can begin loading the website).

You will likely edit and update your website many times as your business evolves. If you feel somewhat confident with experimenting with software (you don't even have to know programming, though it helps of course), it is actually not difficult to learn how to customize your website, especially if you already have the general template to work with. There is software that lets you import your website, edit and modify it, save it to your computer, and put it back to the server: Adobe Dreamweaver (for PC or Mac) is an excellent choice for this because it is intuitive and can show you what the website looks like as you edit it (called "what you see is what you get," or WYSIWYG software). It also easily lets you upload new documents to the server for others to view on the website or for downloading. Even if you have someone build a customized website for you, it is still worth having this software so that you can make your own updates and edits as time goes on, rather than having to call a website programmer every time you need an update.

To use web editing software like Dreamweaver, you will need to have your HTTP address (e.g., http://www.innovatorguide.com), site name (e.g., innovatorguide.com), hosting server login name and password, and you will need to ask your hosting company for the FTP Hosting address (e.g., biz.inmotionhosting.com) and host directory (e.g., /public_html/). You then designate a root folder on your computer where all your website information can be stored (and which also creates a backup of your website information in the case of hackers or viruses). If your host does not provide web building software with your account, you can buy pre-built website templates, then edit and load them through any software that can run a file transfer process (FTP), using the settings as described above.

WordPress is an alternative option for website building—it is well-known and easy to use, but is typically used more for simple blog-type websites. There are many other software options for building and editing a website, each of which has advantages and disadvantages—some examples that are similar to Dreamweaver include CoffeCup Software (for PC, free version available), KompoZer (free, open source, for PC), The Escapers Flux (for Mac), Panic Coda (for Mac), Microsoft FrontPage (for PC), Microsoft Expression Studio (for PC), ActiveState Komodo (for PC or Mac), and many others.

If you are not a programmer and you need more complex features in a website, or if your core business idea involves a new website functionality or unique online service, you will need professional website programmers to get it up and running. Such services may include cloud-based applications, e-commerce sites, social media sites, or many others. For websites with very high volume traffic you may need to consider VPS hosting or dedicated servers.

In addition, hosting services allow you to create email addresses with your website (e.g., info@innovatorguide.com), thereby allowing you to receive and send emails either through the website host or via an email manager like Microsoft Outlook or directly from a smartphone. The email account is typically setup using IMAP, you just need your account login information and your mail server address, often something like mail.innovatorguide.com (you can also use POP settings but this deletes the emails from the server when they download to the computer or phone).

Internet Presence – Graphic Design

Logos should clearly show your company name and preferably some identifying symbol, either separate from or integrated into the text. It may be wise to have a couple versions of logos for various needs, such as one with the text of the company name alone, and another with only a design logo, and perhaps a third that incorporates both. These can be used for websites, business cards, letterhead, emails, products, packaging, marketing, and many other needs.

Many graphic artists can create a professional company logo for quite cheap. Local graphic designers often look for work on LinkedIn or Craigslist, as well as on freelance websites such as www.elance.com, which is an inexpensive source of graphic designers who post their portfolios and make competing bids for your project. This not only pushes down costs (usually around $30 per logo, depending on complexity), but also allows you to explain your exact project needs, review the portfolios of many artists, and only pay when you are satisfied with the final outcome.

Adobe Illustrator is very useful for graphic logo design. In fact, as a side note, the entire Adobe Creative Suite is a package of software that is extremely beneficial for any company. It includes Dreamweaver (for creating and editing websites), Photoshop (image editing), Illustrator (for creating a variety of logos, vector images, design documents, diagrams, and patent drawings), Flash (for creating interactive flash animations), and InDesign (for creating professional documents, publications, flyers, and brochures). Sometimes previous versions like CS4 instead of CS5 can be found more cheaply and work just as well). This software is extremely useful for editing a variety of websites, logos, images, documents, PDF files, tables, figures, brochures, etc. If you do not have your own image editing software, you should be sure to obtain your logos from your graphic designer in the following formats: .ai, .pdf, .png, .gif, and .jpg. PNG files, for example, have many advantages, including the ability to utilize clear backgrounds (rather than white), and they can provide a professional look with low file size in a wide variety of situations, such as a websites, PowerPoint presentations, or grant applications. Vector files (like .ai and .pdf files) allow easy manipulation and expansion of the image with no loss in resolution.

The following is a visual example of a text logo and a symbol logo created in Adobe Illustrator. The text logo was created using the text tool, then using the "create outlines" function to convert the text into an image. The text image of SKYENTIA® was then copied and inverted, making a reflected shadow using the "linear gradient" function to fade the letters. Similarly, the image logo was created using the circle tool to draw simple circles and semicircles, and a neuron image was outlined into the circle. In just a couple clicks of the mouse, the "radial gradient" function was then used on the circles to add shading and create a spherical aspect to the image, and the image was submitted for design trademark.

Internet Presence – Search Engine Optimization (SEO)

Once you have your website up (or at least a draft), you should register the URL (e.g., http://www.innovatorguide.com) with search engines so that it starts showing up in web searches and earning rank priority. You can search for the URL submission sites for each search engine, or use the links below to submit your website to the major search engines:

> Google: https://www.google.com/webmasters/tools/submit-url
> Bing: http://www.bing.com/toolbox/webmaster/
> Yahoo: http://search.yahoo.com/info/submit.html
> (Yahoo will soon integrate with Bing)

You can also visit the Google Dashboard (or Bing Webmaster tools) to complete many useful web and business functions: see http://www.google.com/submityourcontent/#. One particularly useful function is Google Analytics, which provides a simple way to monitor all your website traffic, including locations from where people are visiting your site, how long they spend on each page, and other valuable information. Google Analytics provides a simple paragraph of JavaScript for your website, which can easily be copied and pasted into the website code, typically right before the end header code (e.g., just before "</head>") on the home or index page (even in websites made from standard templates). This can be done in any website code editor, like Adobe Dreamweaver discussed previously.

The ability of your website to show up in internet searches is enhanced by search engine optimization (SEO). Going back, this is actually another reason that you should choose a unique name for your company, since unique words will be far more likely to move up the ladder of internet visibility. Although there are many SEO companies who can work to enhance your website traffic and visibility, there are actually many ways to enhance internet presence for no cost through a variety of techniques.

One simple method is to register your company's biography or description on websites such as LinkedIn and Manta, or even by creating a Facebook page, as well as on other sites that pertain to your industry and products. Registering with Facebook and Google is free, and also allows open access to popular social media outlets for advertising a company and its products for quite cheap (e.g., you only pay for when people click on an ad, usually ~$1 per click). Many times Facebook and Google provide free gift certificates to their corporate registrants that allow an ad to run for free for a certain number of clicks. Additionally, you can register with Google Adwords and Merchant Center if you plan to have online sales, and Google Adsense if you want to earn money by displaying others' ads on your website.

The company should also make an effort to issue press releases of significant milestones and accomplishments, either through a press-release agency, a public relations firm, or through independent efforts. To do this, you can simply email news websites and blogs that tend to report news specific to your industry, or even email reporters and bloggers who typically write on topics in your field, many of whom are happy to publish interesting information that will increase their readership. For any milestones and accomplishments that demonstrate advancing potential of your company, you can also email business news websites and blogs, although these have a tendency to favor public companies since investors tend to read about companies that they can trade. These types of postings can greatly improve website traffic.

Most web development companies would have charged several thousand dollars to get to this point, but using these strategies you can accomplish this for a mere fraction of the cost.

Staffing

Hiring employees is a first big step for any company. In any business, hiring assistance can make life much easier, but also brings with it new administrative tasks. An office manager, for example, can vastly improve efficiency, allowing the founders to shift their focus to their primary work and away from administrative tasks. No matter the field, whether basic research, engineering, or a medical practice, a good office manager can assist immensely by doing the billing, bookkeeping, documentation, printing, appointments, organization, and other administrative work.

As noted under the *Tax & Accounting* section, early in the life of the company it is advantageous to hire consultants and contracted/temp workers rather than full-time employees if there is a concern about long-term financing or viability. However, be mindful to not take advantage of temporary or contracted workers—state and federal laws dictate that any worker might be considered a full-time employee under certain circumstances, depending, for example, on the number of hours worked, length of employment, the scope of the work, and the compensation provided. Of note, for SBIR/STTR grants (discussed later in much more detail), you do not need to have hired the personnel for the project before submitting the proposal.

When hiring full-time employees or assembling a board for your company, make sure that you recruit high-quality people who are not only intelligent and hard-working but who share your vision and work philosophy, and who can bring experience, connections, camaraderie, and wisdom to help guide the company. It is not necessary to form a board early on, and in fact, it is usually better to wait until the company develops into the later stages of maturity before forming a board, since you will want to recruit high-quality people who can contribute wisdom, mentorship, networking, and resources to the company. Furthermore, if seeking investment funding, the investors will have their own specific preferences in a board. Some executive services can even be temporarily contracted, like an interim Chief Financial Officer (CFO) for temporary services such as setting up a financial accounting system, determining financing needs for reaching certain milestones, or helping to create financial projections that potential investors may want to see (described later in the book).

As you meet people at meetings, conferences, and presentations, keep a sense of people who may be helpful to your endeavor. You may ask them for assistance in the future, and connections to the right people matter. Also consult with experts in your field, such as mentors in industry and academics, since this can add reputability to your endeavor, even if they just provide an advisory role or letters of support for grant applications. These people can be a powerful factor and are often proud to have helped with a company's success. You should also get an idea of a law firm or attorney that you can retain for any future legal advice or assistance; this should obviously be someone with experience both in business law and in your particular specialty or field.

Once you start hiring employees, you must consider whether certain regulations apply, such as workers compensation insurance, unemployment insurance, health insurance, FMLA, and other requirements that are usually based on the total number of employees that the company employs. States usually require that new hiring be reported to the state's new hire reporting registry. In some cases you may also need to register for unemployment tax and worker's compensation insurance, depending on state laws and the nature of the work. The *Tax and Accounting* section has more information on these topics.

Be careful not to grow your organization's staffing too quickly; most products take longer to bring to market than expected, particularly in the technology industry, and unnecessarily burning through capital before having revenue or profit can kill a good idea. Conversely, you also need talented and skilled people who can help bring the technology to market, so each company will have its own balance.

When hiring employees, a company must consider whether a contractual agreement with certain employees is in the company's interest. Most companies do not need a binding agreement with employees, but such agreements can be used to recruit better talent and, more importantly, to prevent disclosure or use of proprietary intellectual property, or to prevent use of a company's system of clients and customers, particularly after the employee no longer works for the company. There have actually been multiple recent instances of these types of problems at large technology companies. Thus non-disclosure agreements and non-compete agreements have become relatively common when innovative and secretive technology is involved.

Facilities

When choosing facilities, plan all your needs and be sure that the building can fulfill these needs. This may include whether you need 3-phase power, high voltage lines, or certain water or gas flows. Also consider logistical aspects such as whether there are there association fees. Also be sure to know who your neighbors are and what their activities are. Also verify that the facility is zoned appropriately for your activities, and whether there are any problems with the location and building. This can save much future stress. In addition, depending on your activities and whether your company is a physical or a virtual one, you should be sure that you are not violating any local zoning and licensing requirements. Light industrial, light manufacturing, and commercial zoning classifications are usually sufficient for most startup companies.

It can sometimes be beneficial to know city/county board members if possible, since they approve building permits and often approve discounts on various fees and taxes for businesses. Permits may be required for working with various types of chemicals or if using any animals or humans in research (in addition to the many other regulatory requirements of animal and human subject research, although most small companies will contract this sort of research with other institutions, as discussed later).

§

PART II – FUNDING

"I returned, and saw under the sun,
that the race is not to the swift,
nor the battle to the strong,
neither yet bread to the wise,
nor yet riches to men of understanding,
nor yet favour to men of skill;
but time and chance happeneth to them all."
Old Testament, Eccl. 9:11.

"I will show you fear in a handful of dust."
T.S. Eliot, *The Waste Land*

Undertaking the quest for funding can be a discouraging process, but it is also a great learning opportunity that will provide valuable tools and insights that help refine your ideas. Much of research and business may be luck, but remember the adage of Louis Pasteur that, "Fortune favors the prepared mind" (University of Lille lecture, 1854).

This is a critical phase for a startup company, and there should be a sense of urgency and careful attention to detail. You will face many critiques and doubts from investors and grant reviewers—use them as constructive advice to improve and refine your idea and approach. They will help reveal potential pitfalls or weaknesses that you had forgotten to consider, and it is better to realize this early on rather than later. Not everyone will understand or believe in you, but nearly every innovator has faced opposition before their success, and as the innovator, you will understand your idea better than anyone, so believe in yourself. At the invention of the phone, the microprocessor, the personal computer, and even planes and rockets, the inventors themselves could not have envisioned the vast and incredible technologies and applications that exist today.

The entrepreneurial founder has a tremendous weight on his or her shoulders. In addition to being creative enough to think of a new idea, the founder must also sacrifice tremendous efforts on intellectual property protection, creating a legal business entity, networking with skilled colleagues, and, perhaps most importantly, securing financing. Because the quest for financing can be so unpredictable, it is sometimes best to take a shotgun approach, using personal funds when necessary but also submitting grant applications to federal agencies and private foundations, as well as continually presenting at investor meetings when the opportunity arises.

There are three basic ways to fund your company: 1) grants (usually non-dilutive funding), 2) equity financing (dilutive investments), and 3) debt financing (usually must be secured with some form of asset-backing). Equity financing may include venture capital investments, angel investments, private equity fund investment, hedge fund investment, crowd-funding, etc. Debt financing may include credit cards, personal loans, lines of credit, commercial bank loans, SBA-backed bank loans, asset-backed loans, factoring, community development loans, or even corporate bonds or mezzanine financing.

The first round of funding is *seed stage* funding, and if possible, should be sufficient to at least hit the next significant milestone, whether that be proof-of-concept, prototype creation, product development, commercial launch, upscaling, etc. Grants are the ideal method of seed stage funding because they advance the company without taking an equity position in the company.

The following sections are divided into the overarching categories of grants first, investment capital second, with discussion of several other methods of financing last.

GRANTS

Grants can be extraordinarily important for a startup company. Grants are one of the best sources of seed funding, bridging the funding gap between an idea and investor interest. The farther you can get with grants in the early stages, the more you can add value to your company, thus giving away less of the company to investors and bringing in more funding than if obtaining investor capital early on.

Grants discussed here are those that do not require payback or ownership of part of the company. These may include SBIR grants, non-profit or private foundations grants, state or community grants, some angel investor grants, economic development initiatives, seed funding organizations, and others. If the research is very early basic science, you may also consider applying for an R21 exploratory grant or even an R01 grant (but this will require competing with the entire academic field for these grants).

More states are beginning to have SBIR matching programs, which match a portion of SBIR federal business grants using state funds. There may also be state and local economic development grants or loan programs. Also consider private and non-profit foundations and institutions. The website http://www.tgci.com/funding.shtml shows major funding foundations by state, or you can search professional societies applicable to your goals—for example, any "American [X] Association" (including Heart, Lung, Stroke, Diabetes, Parkinson's, etc.) may fund correlative research and technology. Many charitable foundations are dedicated to solving certain sets of problems, and they typically post funding opportunities on their websites. Grants and funding opportunities change each year, but one of the most consistent resources for small businesses is the SBIR/STTR program.

SBIR/STTR Grants

SBIR/STTR grants can be a great benefit to business, both for funding purposes and for gaining recognition and credibility. These non-dilutive grants take no ownership in the technology or company, and they do not require any repayment. Thus these grants can provide seed funding for a startup company and can also attract investors, partnerships, and customers. Congress requires that federal agencies with research budgets over $100 million must spend 2.5% of their budget on the small business innovation research (SBIR) grants in the United States, and 0.3% on small business technology transfer (STTR) grants. This includes 11 agencies of government, shown in Table 1, and comprises over $2 billion in annual funding, with approximately half being spent through the Department of Defense alone. In the reauthorization of the SBIR program in 2012, the percentage of funding for SBIR will gradually increase to 3.2% by 2017. These grants are used to fund a wide variety of technologies and projects.

Table 1: The departments of government that participate in SBIR grants. The first five are also required to fund STTR (excluding the FDA and CDC):
1. Department of Defense (DOD)
2. Department of Energy (DOE)
3. Department of Health and Human Services (HHS)
    [includes the National Institutes of Health (NIH), the Food and Drug Administration (FDA), the Centers for Disease Control (CDC), and the Agency for Healthcare Research and Quality (AHRQ)]
4. National Aeronautics and Space Administration (NASA)
5. National Science Foundation (NSF)
6. Environmental Protection Agency (EPA)
7. Department of Education (ED)
8. Department of Homeland Security (DHS)
9. Department of Transportation (DOT)
10. Department of Agriculture (USDA)
11. Department of Commerce (DOC)
    [includes the National Oceanic and Atmospheric Administration and the National Institute of Standards and Technology]

Typical limits in funding for SBIR grants are $150k for phase I (6 months in length) and $1 million for phase II (2 years in length). Limits for STTR are typically $100k for phase I (12 months) and $750k for phase II (2 years). Some agencies are able to award more time and/or money than these limits (see below). Phase I is meant to show feasibility and phase II is to complete research and development and prepare for commercialization. A phase II competing/continuing-renewal award (phase IIB) may also be available, which can provide an additional $3 million over 3 years to aid regulatory approval and commercialization of the technology.

Applications can also be submitted as a combined phase I/phase II project (called a fast-track application), but this should usually be reserved for applicants who have experience in obtaining SBIR grants because of the substantial amount of preparation and expertise required. This track allows phase I funding that automatically leads to phase II funding with the submission of a satisfactory phase I report.

In order to be eligible for these grants, the small business must be an U.S. owned, independently operated, for-profit organization with 500 employees or less. The STTR is designed to help technologies created at U.S. universities and non-profit research organizations to come to market through small businesses, and the SBIR is designed to help technologies that are created or developed by small businesses. Thus for the SBIR, the principal researcher must be employed by the company, work at least 51% of time on the project, and not be employed full-time elsewhere, whereas for the STTR the principal researcher can be employed by the university or other non-profit institution. The STTR requires that at least 30% of the award fund collaborative work at the non-profit institution and at least 40% of the work be done by the small business, whereas the SBIR allows a company to collaborate with a university at will, with the university doing no more than 33% in phase I or 50% in phase II.

Such collaboration with other institutions may require a sub-award agreement, but if the contributions of the university collaboration are minor, it is easier to simply contract university facilities or services and to list university professors as consultants. Universities typically already have their own standardized sub-award agreement forms, so you will likely need to make negotiations based on those. Universities and institutions will likely also have indemnification agreements and assignment of ownership agreements for new discoveries. For sub-award agreements, a template that meets federal guidelines can be found at http://sites.nationalacademies.org/PGA/fdp/PGA_063626.

It should be noted that the government does not typically allow the awardee company to take ownership of intellectual property created by the sub-contractor as a condition of awarding the contract to the sub-contractor. This can be a significant issue, but the company and the sub-contractor are allowed to negotiate any agreement of ownership of potential intellectual property, just technically not as a condition of awarding the sub-contract. Please see the information under the *Intellectual Property under SBIR/STTR* and *Non-Disclosure Agreement* sections for more information about issues of ownership under these agreements and grants.

Of note, the difference between a consultant and a subcontractor basically depends on who is giving the directions: if a university professor is conducting their own portion of research, the professor is considered a subcontractor, whereas if a professor is hired to provide input or complete a specific task, then the professor can be considered a consultant. A subcontractor necessitates a sub-award contract, whereas a consultant can simply list an hourly cost rate with an estimated total number of hours to be contributed. It is advantageous to have consultants consisting of experts in the field, whether from university or private industry, even if just to show that the grant recipient will have expert help available in case there is a project failure or barrier.

Previously venture capital could only own less than 50% of the company in order to be eligible for SBIR/STTR. With the reauthorization of the SBIR/STTR program, however, grant eligibility has been proposed to broaden to companies that may be majority-owned by venture capitalists, with the limitation that federal agencies cannot allocate more than 15% of their SBIR funds to these companies. In addition, the reauthorization of the SBIR program funding is proposed to increase to $150,000 for phase I and up to $1 million for phase II. In certain cases, phase I funding may actually exceed this amount (for example, the NIH allows phase I funding up to $350,000 per year for up to two years), but all budget components must be justified. It also appears in the reauthorization that phase II awards may be granted without a previous phase I award and may be renewable. It should also be noted that if you need extensions of time to complete the work and file reports, you may have up to a year to continue work after funding ends and then file a final report. This may be beneficial if you are hoping to make a good impression from a phase I award and need more time to complete all milestones, and gives more time to prepare a phase II application. For those who obtain SBIR/STTR awards, other services and resources will also be made available to the business, such as "niche assessment," "commercialization assistance," and matchmaking of strategic partners and investors.

Agencies list the research and work that they are interested in funding in an *omnibus* each year. These contain funding opportunity announcements ("FOA" or "solicitations"), which can be broad or very specific (the more specific project solicitations tend to have more strict deadlines, particularly with the DOD, whereas the broader opportunities can typically be submitted at various deadlines throughout the year, such as with the NIH). Thus some agencies may give very specific milestones and goals for each phase of the project, while others may allow you to set your own milestones and goals for the project. Occasionally, some project solicitations may also request that you send a short 'letter of intent' to the program director prior to the submission of a formal application.

Open solicitations for all agencies and departments can be found at http://www.grants.gov/ and http://www.sbir.gov/solicitations (or http://www.zyn.com/sbir/). Agencies and departments also have their own websites for SBIR funding opportunities, and it is good to review their omnibus solicitation to understand the primary objectives of the grant funding, the variations in funding or due dates, and where your project might best fit. Note that the websites for each agency's funding opportunities can vary: the DOD small business solicitations are listed at http://www.dodsbir.net/solicitation/ and also at http://www.acq.osd.mil/osbp/sbir/index.shtml, while those for the NIH are at http://grants.nih.gov/grants/funding/sbir.htm. A broader listing of federal funding and contracts is http://www.cfda.gov/, but this includes some obsolete, unfunded ("non-obligated") programs. You can search all these sites by topic or keyword, and it is useful to do this to see the abundance and variety in funding opportunities, which may give you many ideas on projects that you could successfully accomplish.

Additionally, you can also submit your own ideas and proposals to certain agencies, either under one of the solicited funding opportunities that best applies to your proposal, or with your own proposal under an "omnibus program solicitation" if it fits with the goals and aims of the agency. Most proposals could theoretically fall under multiple funding opportunities within the same department (e.g., similar solicitations from the National Cancer Institute), or under similar funding opportunities from different divisions or institutes (e.g., similarly applicable solicitations from the NINDS and NIBIB), or even amongst multiple different agencies or departments (e.g., research

27

may be simultaneously applicable to the Department of Defense, the National Science Foundation, and the National Institutes of Health). In these cases, you should pick the best agency, which should be judged by several criteria, such as whether they typically fund similar work, whether they have the best expertise to judge your project, and where they rank in terms of funding amounts. This last question is pertinent, because each agency, institute, or department has only a certain amount of funding. The following tables (Tables 2 and 3) rank the departments and subdivisions by funding available.

Table 2: Ranking of departments by funding amounts. (From 13th Annual NIH SBIR/STTR Conference, June 22-23, 2011, Bethesda, MD.)

1.	DOD	5.	NSF	9.	ED
2.	HHS	6.	DHS	10.	EPA
3.	NASA	7.	USDA	11.	DOT
4.	DOE	8.	DOC		

Table 3: Ranking of National Institutes of Health by funding amounts (the first four controlled 50% of the total $680 million in NIH SBIR/STTR funding in 2011. Also note that the SBIR budgets of the CDC, FDA, and AHRQ are less than 2% of the funding of the NIH). (From 13th Annual NIH SBIR/STTR Conference, June 22-23, 2011, Bethesda, MD.)

1.	NCI	9.	NICHD	17.	NIDCD
2.	NIAID	10.	NIA	18.	NIDCR
3.	NHLBI	11.	NIDA	19.	NIBIB
4.	NIDDK	12.	NEI	20.	NCMHD
5.	NIGMS	13.	NIEHS	21.	NINR
6.	NINDS	14.	NIAMS	22.	NCCAM
7.	NIMH	15.	NHGRI	23.	NLM
8.	NCRR	16.	NIAAA		

It should be noted that applications may actually be submitted to different agencies for similar work, but only one award may be accepted, meaning that if work is duplicated in the applications, it can only be funded by one agency. Programs directors for various agencies are usually happy to talk to you (emails are best, with contact information available on the agency websites) before submission of a proposal to advise whether an application best fits with the agency's objectives and interests.

States sometimes have their own small business assistance centers, which often charge a fee for providing assistance and information on SBIR/STTR applications. The information offered is likely not any more detailed or helpful than what can be found on the websites of the funding agencies. On the other hand, conferences on SBIR/STTR grant opportunities are sometimes conducted by the funding agencies themselves, and these tend to be much more informative. These conferences may be held annually and may offer the opportunity to visit and speak with the directors personally. You can also consider subscribing to an agency's email list (if available) for updates on grant opportunities, requirements, updates, and deadlines.

Due dates vary by agency, and some opportunities have recurring deadlines, while other solicitations might have only one specific due date. General SBIR deadlines at the NIH are April 5, August 5, and December 5 each year, whereas the DOD deadlines are usually in June and September of each year. It typically takes about 4-6 months to know the final funding status of the application. In some cases, you may receive critiques a couple weeks before the next recurring deadline, in which case you may be able to revise the application in time for the next deadline. Such revisions may include adding additional letters of support, adding preliminary data, revising protocols, further defining applications and benefits of your technology, and addressing other critiques. However, some critiques may require significantly more time to address. Many agencies only allow an SBIR grant to be revised once, so it is more important to take the time to carefully address all possible critiques rather than rush the revision. After 37 months, however, applications can be considered "new" again, even if not revised.

Only the top ~50% of applications are discussed in review groups and given a priority score, where a lower score is better. For example, at the NIH, a score of 100 to 200 is almost always funded, a score of 200-300 is sometimes funded, and ~50% of applications in the 300-500 range are not given a final score (unscored). This score is derived from individual category ratings of significance, expertise, innovation, approach, and environment, and each category is given a score of 1-10, averaged amongst the reviewers, then summed and multiplied by 10. Recent funding rates for phase I applications are about 15-20%, and this rate is about the same for fast-track applications. Success rates for phase II applications are higher, about 33-45%, depending on the agency.

Almost all grant applicants have applications rejected at some point, which can be very discouraging, especially considering all the effort and thought involved in constructing the application. Even well-known experts and experienced grant writers have had applications rejected, so do not be discouraged. Due to the competitive nature, even innovative and meaningful projects can be rejected if the reviewers have unfavorable opinions or critiques of any aspect of the project. In the revision, it is best not to mount overt arguments to the reviewers' concerns unless there is significant evidence to support the premise, but rather to revise accordingly, polishing all aspects to be as professional and well-supported as possible, and then state in the cover letter that the amended application contains significant revisions that satisfy the concerns and critiques of the previous review. Even if funding is denied in a revision, there are several examples of companies that became very successful despite rejection of funding and grants.

You must register your company with each agency you wish to apply to, and each agency is has its own system. Registration with each agency will require both an EIN and DUNS number. You should also register with http://grants.gov, where most grant applications will be submitted, as well as with http://ccr.gov, which will document the nature of your business, including NAICS/SIC codes applicable to the goods and services your company can provide, and these can be updated at any time. Registration should be done as early as possible because it can take weeks for all processing to occur. Of note, the ccr.gov website will likely migrate to the new sam.gov system sometime in 2013. A DUNS number is required for all companies receiving or requesting funds from the government. The fastest way to obtain this is by calling D&B at 888-347-0475 or go to www.dnb.com. This is a rare instance where a phone call is much easier and faster than online registration, but D&B will also try to get you to subscribe to credit services for your company—there is no need to sign up for any of the services or payments associated with the DUNS number registration.

Agencies require registration through their individual systems. For the DOD, register at http://www.dodsbir.net/submission/SignIn.asp. For the DHHS & NIH, the business must be registered in eRA Commons at commons.era.nih.gov. Within the eRA system, the small-business, the principal investigator (PI), and the authorized signing official (SO/AOR) must each be registered (two different logins are still required even if the AOR and the PI are the same person). The PI submits the application while the AOR must approve it for submission. The funding opportunity description and grant application forms are usually PDF files that can be downloaded from the www.grants.gov website or from the funding agency itself. The completed application is then submitted either directly from a link in the PDF file (through grants.gov), or through the specific agency's website. Always be sure to verify proper submission and receipt of your application.

Each agency also provides specific instructions on how to put together a grant application, including formats and all components required. The SF424 form, for example, is the main form for the grant application through a number of agencies, such as the NIH (replacing the prior Public Health Service grant form PHS 398). It is a simple PDF to which all submission materials are attached, which may include an introduction, abstract, aims, narrative, research strategy (6 pages for phase I, 12 pages for phase II), references, human or animal study protocols, budgets, letters, equipment and facilities descriptions, and/or commercialization plan (all described in further detail below). Specific instructions can be found from the submission site of each agency, and each application form has a separate form of detailed instructions. The instructions for the SF424 form are available at http://grants.nih.gov/grants/funding/424/index.htm.

For human or animal research, a company does not need to have its own clinics or animal research facilities. In fact, it is likely financially beneficial to contract these services with a university's core facilities or with private research institutions, since such facilities can require significant personnel and resources. Assurances for research will still need to be given to the applicant company even when contracting a facility that already has assurances (for example, the small business must still acquire its own OLAW assurance if conducting animal research), but this can be done through an inter-institutional assurance between the small business, the NIH, and the contracted lab, and this can be obtained after announcement of the award announcement but prior to receipt of funds. This is done according to the SF424 instructions, by indicating that an IRB and/or IACUC review will be pending, that there is not yet an animal welfare assurance number, and that you will fulfill the "Just-in-Time" requirement by submitting the applicable human subjects or animal welfare assurance before the funds are released.

All animal research must assure the welfare and humane treatment of all animals. Animal study protocols must therefore address five points: 1) details of the proposed use of animals, with species, strains, ages, sex, and numbers, 2) justification of these choices, 3) details on the veterinary care of the animals, 4) detailed methods of minimizing pain and distress in all stages of animal use, and 5) methods of euthanasia and compliance with AVMA standards (see the Vertebrate Animals Section checklist at http://grants.nih.gov/grants/olaw/VASchecklist.pdf). For human subjects, the protocol must address protection of human subjects from research risks, data and safety monitoring plan, and contain a plan for inclusion of women, minorities, and children. Further details on required components of research protocols for human subjects research or for vertebrate animals research can be found in 21 CFR 50 or in SF424 instructions at http://grants.nih.gov/grants/funding/424/index.htm. Also see *Part IV – Regulatory Issues* for more detailed information.

Writing the Grant

The grant review committees see thousands of applications, so it is important to capture their attention as soon as possible. They will likely first skim over the title, the abstract, then maybe the background of the applicant. Therefore it is essential to make sure that the title of the application contains both the "problem" (the significance) and the "product" (the innovation). For example, "A Novel [Technology] for Improved [Purpose]" makes a strong title. This gives the grant reviewers the quickest impression of why they should pay attention to your application.

The rest of the application should tell a compelling story about why your proposal is innovative and meaningful. As mentioned previously, the application is typically assessed on the factors below (with different names amongst the different agencies for similar criteria):

- Innovation/Scientific Merit
- Significance/Impact
- Approach/Feasibility/Effectiveness/Commercial Merit
- Expertise/Qualifications/Experience
- Resources/Equipment/Facilities/Business Environment

The agencies also assign different weight to the different components. The most important aspect in the application itself is to make a clear argument for the significance of the problem you are tackling and the unique benefit and novelty of your solution and approach. Be specific in the benefits your technology will provide.

Also important are the specific methods used in the project, the expertise and resources of the team, and the market potential of the idea, any one of which could be cause for rejection. In other words, you must make a convincing argument for the impact of the idea, the specific technical approach you will use, and your ability to accomplish it. The technology itself does not necessarily need to be novel; novelty can also be in the creation of a new method or approach to a common technology.

The background of the problem should be described in such a way that it demonstrates expert knowledge of the field. You should include detailed references to important and recent work in the field while still maintaining brevity so that the examiner can get to the more important parts of the application. The ability to accomplish the idea is reinforced by a detailed background, a detailed methodology, as well as by the biosketches (résumés or CVs) of the investigators. The backgrounds of the investigators should show convincing evidence that they are the right experts to perform the proposed work. It is alright if all the staff have not yet been hired as long as they will be ready to work once the project is funded.

The project summary should be brief, certainly less than one page, and will often be given length limitations by the agency. This summary should describe in relatively detailed terms the aims and objectives of project, why it is important or significant, and specific and measureable milestones. The narrative is used in some agencies to briefly describe (typically ≤3 sentences) in plain language the public impact and relevance of the project.

The research strategy or project description should be a compelling, detailed, and professionally-written description of the significance, innovation, and approach of the project, often with an introduction or background of the problem and prior work, a solution proposal, and detailed approach and methods. The problem does not need to be a problem in the literal sense of the word, but can also represent an opportunity for improvement. It should reference important and current literature in the field that supports the background, innovation, and feasibility of the idea. Also include any preliminary work or data, as well as statistical methods to be employed in data analysis.

The proposal should include at least one good image or diagram that represents the project and its goals, preferably a well-made graphic image (as mentioned above, graphic artwork can be contracted through elance.com or made with software such as Adobe Illustrator, etc.). It is also helpful to include an image that shows the general timeline of the milestones in the project.

Grant opportunities with specific timelines and specifications are rather easy to organize and write, but open grant opportunities can be more difficult to organize, since you must figure out a timeline that is neither to long nor too short to accomplish the proposed work. If setting your own milestones, be specific, and describe how you will achieve them and how you will measure success or completion of the milestones. You must set milestones that show measurable accomplishments and reasonable steps towards feasibility and commercialization. Talking to agency administrators about your proposal before submission can be beneficial in these situations.

Unlike typical scientific grants, which are hypothesis-driven, SBIR/STTR grants are product-driven. All agencies seek to fund work that has commercialization potential, i.e., work that will fill meaningful market needs or government needs. In phase I, commercialization strategies may be brief or not required at all, but all agencies will request detailed commercialization strategies for phase II and beyond. See the *Commercialization* section for more information.

Agencies report common reasons for rejection to be not having a particularly significant or innovative idea, not having commercial potential, unclear or concerning research plan, unclear milestones or tests of feasibility, lack of expertise, too early-stage/high-risk research, and lack of letters of support from collaborators, contractors, or supporting experts in the field.

The following table (Table 4) shows general components of an application, including components needed in DOD, DOE, HHS, NIH, NSF, NASA, and other applications (with different names amongst the different agencies for similar sections). The subheadings under "Research Strategy" are possible subheadings that may be used in a proposal, but note that some agencies may request these components to be submitted as separate documents rather than one combined project description.

SBIR/STTR Components

Table 4: Outline of SBIR/STTR components.
- Company Information
- Investigator Information
- Project Summary/Abstract*
- Narrative/Public Benefits*
- Aims/Milestones*
- Research Strategy/Project Description/Technical Proposal
  - Problem/Significance
  - Solution/Innovation
  - Technical Objectives/Aims/Milestones
  - Technical Approach/Work Plan/Protocol/Methods
  - Anticipated Results/Assessment
  - Summary/Future Plans/Future Applications/Impact/Etc.
- Budget
- Contractual Agreements (Consultants/Subcontractors)
- Cooperative Agreements for STTR
- Letters of Support/Commitment
- Equipment Description
- Facilities Description
- Vertebrate Animals
- Human Studies
- References/Bibliography
- Key Personnel/Biosketches/Backgrounds/Experience/Expertise
- Related/Pending/Similar Applications
- Progress Report (if continuing a previously funded project)

* = Only required by some agencies separate from the project description itself.

A cover letter is optional for new applications, but typically required for revised applications. The agency itself will assign the application to the institute or review group that best fits with the scope of the application unless the cover letter requests a specific review group within the agency. More specifically, the cover letter can request assignment to an institute: for example, as when multiple sponsoring institutes are listed on a funding opportunity announcement), or to a specific review group within an institute (such as the many scientific review groups (SRGs) or integrated review groups (IRGs) of the NIH found at http://public.csr.nih.gov/StudySections/IntegratedReviewGroups/Pages/defaul t.aspx. The cover letter can also identify any specific expertise needed or possible conflicts of interest in the review group members.

The project description itself should be generally be written in either Arial or Helvetica font, at least size 11pt, with at least half inch margins, although these specific requirements may vary from agency to agency.

To summarize, some general tips include:
- Review the specific SBIR instructions for your agency
- Include figures and timelines with your proposal
- Make the project title and summary clear, focusing on benefits of your technology, useful applications, specific goals and milestones, and the feasibility of success.
- Emphasize the novelty and innovation of your technology and approach
- Discuss possible weaknesses and failure points of your proposal. If you do not, the reviewers will find them anyway and the failure to address them will raise concerns.
- Obtain letters of support from those who are experts in the field who can offer their support and validate your approach and the need for the work.
- Contact the federal agency before applying to ensure that your application best fits within the aims of that agency (each agency has a listed contact person whom you can email).
- Discuss commercialization of your technology (even in phase I applications, at least briefly mention it; phase II applications require it, and you should make it as thorough and detailed as possible, including market analysis and letters of support from possible purchasers, vendors, manufacturers, partnerships, etc.).

Budget & Accounting

Grant awards are determined on scientific merit rather than budgeting, but a good budget shows that you have expertise to handle the project and that you have thought through all the specific aspects that will be needed to complete the objectives of the project. The budget of course can change in the course of the work. You must justify the budget of course, but do not be afraid to request all that is needed. The concepts below may seem tedious, but they are important for any business owner to understand.

When documenting expenses under a grant, each expense or cost must be categorized as "Direct," "Indirect," or "Unallowable." This can be done in a variety of ways, whether in a simple data entry format or in accounting software (see the *Tax and Accounting* section). Each funded project should be documented separately, including all labor and expenses. Be sure to keep all time sheets, payroll slips, invoices, and receipts. Table 5 shows examples of how costs should be categorized in an SBIR/STTR grant budget:

Table 5: Categorization of costs in SBIR/STTR accounting.
1. **Direct Costs**
    a. General Direct Costs
        i. Salaries
        ii. Materials/Supplies (directly related to the funded project)
        iii. Equipment*
        iv. Consultants
        v. Travel
        vi. Subawards (if <$25,000)
    b. Fringe§ (generally calculated as 25% of salaries)
        i. Paid Time Off
        ii. Payroll Taxes
        iii. 401(k) Plan
        iv. Health Insurance
2. **Indirect Costs** (Phase I≤40% of direct costs, Phase II=negotiated rate)
    a. Manager/Administrator/Executive Salaries
    b. Bookkeeping
    c. Accounting
    d. Facilities Lease/Mortgage

e. Utilities

f. General Supplies (not directly related to the funded project, e.g., office supplies)

g. Legal Costs

h. Subawards (if >$25,000)

3. **Unallowable Costs**

a. Debt

b. Interest

c. Donations

d. Expenses for other company-funded projects[+]

* Equipment can count as direct cost, but when negotiating an "indirect cost rate" for phase II grants (see below), equipment is excluded from prior direct costs in the calculation. The definition of equipment is typically a non-expendable piece of property with a cost ≥$5000 (or sometimes less). Therefore, it is good to keep equipment and subawards separately labeled in record-keeping.

§ The inclusion of fringe costs as a direct cost is perfectly allowable, and is called a "two-tier system." Fringe costs can be listed as indirect costs if you so choose ("one-tier system"), but this would provide much less total funding for the same work.

+ Internal R&D, unrelated to the funded project, is unallowable for grant accounting purposes, but may be included as a direct cost in the "indirect cost rate" negotiation.

Companies can request salaries for personnel directly involved in the project, and as shown above, salaries count as direct costs. Indirect costs include facility and administrative (F&A) costs. For phase I grants, indirect costs are typically calculated as 35-40% of direct costs, with no justification required. In phase II, the indirect cost rate is "negotiated" by the funding agency, and is typically based on actual indirect costs of the company relative to direct costs (and typically amounts to less than 40% of direct costs). This negotiation usually takes place at the end of the first year of a phase II grant, using the first year to obtain actual costs and expenses. The company can also request a corporate profit (also called a "fee") of up to a maximum 7%, calculated as 7% of total costs (direct + indirect).

As a simple example, let's say you are the sole worker on a one year project and you want an annual salary of $80,000, and you anticipate spending 90% of your time directly on the project. You have calculated the costs of all materials and supplies to be $50,000. You would take $80,000 * .90 = $72,000 for the salary request. $72,000 * .25 = $18,000 for fringe costs. Therefore $72,000 + $18,000 = $90,000 in direct costs for salary, plus $50,000 direct costs for materials, equals $140,000 in total direct allowable costs. Indirect costs are calculated as $140,000 * .40 = $56,000. The total funding then is $140,000 +

$56,000 = $196,000. With a 7% profit, the company may then submit a total budget request of $209,720.

You should maintain a labor documentation system that can account for labor hours, and that can categorize the labor. This can be done with software such as Google EchoSign. All time worked on an SBIR/STTR funded project must be tracked, and similar to accounting for costs, should be categorized as either "direct," "indirect," or "other." "Direct time" refers to time spent directly on the funded project (also called "billable hours"). "Indirect time" refers to other work not pertaining to the project, such as administrative tasks or other research work. "Other time" should document paid time off (PTO) as well as unpaid time off. Indirect costs are not assignable to a grant, but rather to the company itself. Time sheets should be signed or verified by both the employee and the supervisor.

Of note, grant regulations base salary on a 40-hour work week. Therefore, for a worker who works 40 hours directly on the project and 20 hours on other tasks, the "effective hourly rate" needs to be recalculated as 40/60 or 66% of direct time to the project. Therefore, a salary of $1500 per week could technically only charge $1000 directly to the project that week. Furthermore, if salary was budgeted at 90% time but is then expected to drop to 66%, this must be reported to the funding agency.

Clearly having professional accounting assistance can be an advantage, particularly under a financial audit. Federal audits are typically not done if the company's funding is less than $500,000 per year. The accountant should be familiar with the principles of an A-133 audit, SBIR/STTR accounting methods, and/or Defense Contract Audit Agency (DCAA) rules for DOD contracts. The audit reassures that you are following the proper accounting principles discussed here. Pitfalls include mis-categorizing costs, inadequately monitoring sub-contractors and sub-awards, and delinquent close-out reporting. Grant recipients are responsible for all sub-recipients, and agreements generally state that the grant recipient is responsible for the financial aspects of the project including all funds appropriated to sub-recipients.

All these policies can seem overwhelming, but do not worry: funding agencies are willing to help with any questions, and any aspects not covered in detail here can usually be figured out as you go or you can contact the funding agency for training materials or for unique issues pertaining to your situation. The funding agency has usually prepared teaching materials or templates, and information can also be found at various offices such as the Division of Grants Compliance and Oversight, the Office of Policy for Extramural Research Operation, the Office of Acquisition Management and Policy, the Defense Finance and Accounting Service, the Office of Management and Budget, or others. If you would like to read details of other regulatory policies on small business grants, such information can be found in 45 CFR parts 74 (administrative), 2 CFR part 215 (administrative), Circular A-110 (administrative), 48 CFR 31.2 (budgeting), 45 CFR part 74.26 (auditing), 42 CFR part 52 (research grant awards), and 45 CFR part 46 (human subjects research), 21 CFR part 50 & 56 (human subjects research and IRB), and the Animal Welfare Act and PHS policy on Humane Care and Use of Laboratory Animals (animal research). Also see further discussions of research protocol design in the *FDA Regulatory Pathways* section later in this book.

Post-Award

Once a grant application is approved, it must also be processed through the Office of Management and Budget, which appropriates the funds. The institution will receive a notice of award, which includes most necessary information for how to obtain the funds and any particular terms or conditions. The funding goes to the institution, not the PI. If the project involves human or animal research, you will need to make sure that any assurances are complete for human or animal research at this time. Agencies may dispense funds through the Division of Payment Management, but each agency will send specific instructions on how funds are to be received. The Division of Payment Management can be found at http://www.dpm.psc.gov/.

As mentioned previously, each funded grant should be maintained as a separate account, and the accounting system, whether paper or digital, should assign expenses of each program by grant and category. Time records should account for all of an employee's hours. All transactions should be supported by documentation. It also helps to show some form of internal control to prevent overspending total funds available for both the overall grant and allottable amounts for each category. The PI and AOR are responsible for grant compliance and oversight (these can be the same person at small businesses), or you can choose to have a financial account administrator. For larger firms, the *books of accounts*, whether manual or digital, may include the appropriate general ledger, project cost ledger, cash receipts journal, cash disbursements journal, payroll journal, accounts receivable ledger, accounts payable ledger, sales journal, and/or purchase journal (see the *Tax & Accounting* section).

Changes may be made to any part of the proposed plan even after the project has begun, but any significant changes need to be approved by or at least disclosed to the funding agency. In particular, if the labor of a subcontractor or consultant changes by more than 25% or if the subcontractor or consultant withdraws from the project or becomes absent >3 months, the grant management office must be given written notice signed by the AOR (email is acceptable). Additionally, if there are significant changes in project scope, aims, methods, costs, equipment, etc., such changes must also be disclosed in writing to the grant management office. Costs incurred 90 days prior to grant funding are also allowable, but must also be requested through the grant management office. Large equipment purchases will always require written approval before purchase (particularly items with costs into the tens of thousands).

If you need extensions of time to complete the project objectives and file a final report, the funding agency will likely allow up to a year extension after funding ends. This may be beneficial to complete all phase I milestones and objectives and have more time to prepare a phase II application.

Additional Resources

The *Technology Innovation Program* (TIP) through the *National Institute of Standards and Technology* (NIST) is a program for small businesses (as well as for universities and large companies), which, similar to SBIR/STTR, is intended to fund innovative research that may have an important impact or that fills critical needs but that may be early stage or high-risk. Notices of these "federal funding opportunities" (FFOs) are announced on both the www.grants.gov website and on www.nist.gov. Unlike SBIR/STTR grants at some other agencies, no unsolicited proposals are allowed. Like SBIR/STTR, proposals are also submitted through www.grants.gov, but funding amounts may reach $3 million for up to 3 years of R&D. Details of how to assemble a proposal are found under the TIP description on the NIST website.

Each federal agency may have several other funding programs for small businesses. *Cooperative Research and Development Agreements* (CRADA), for example, allow federally-funded institutions to assist private entities on research that fulfills objectives of both parties. This may include funding of laboratory space, equipment, or personnel. The federally-funded institution may also allow assignment of rights of intellectual property to the private company. Details can be found on each agency's website.

Some resources of the HHS-NIH for small businesses include services offered by the new *National Center for Advancing Translational Sciences* (NCATS). This center was recently created in recognition of the significant funding gaps between basic science and clinical applications, and it incorporates the previous National Center for Research Resources. The center provides funding resources that include the *Clinical and Translational Science Awards* (CTSAs) and the TRND/CAN/BrIDGs programs (*Therapeutics for Rare and Neglected Diseases, Cures Acceleration Network*, and *Bridging Interventional Development Gaps*, formerly known as RAID). The TRND, CAN, and BrIDGs programs fund various stages of pharmaceutical discovery, including target validation, assay development, lead optimization, pre-clinical development, and early clinical studies of new drugs to help advance more therapeutics for rare and neglected diseases, and more information on these specific programs can be found on the website http://nctt.nih.gov/. The CAN program specifically funds translational research for high-need cures that are otherwise unlikely to be pursued by biotech companies, and these grants may be distributed with or without partnering institutions. Active funding announcements may be called *requests for application* (RFAs), *program announcements* (PAs), *funding opportunity announcements* (FOAs), *solicitations, awards*, etc., which can be found at the HHS grants site by name or by topic: http://grants.nih.gov/grants/guide/index.html.

Other grants may also fund clinical trials, such as RFA awards or the R34 grant. There may also be certain tax grants through the IRS for R&D in many industries such as biotechnology, healthcare, national defense, aerospace, clean energy, etc., but these tax grants tend to have specific criteria that change from year to year.

Certain agencies within the NIH seek to fund the translational gap that exists between academic research and industry development. The NINDS, for example, has the *Blueprint Neurotherapeutics Network* (BPN), which provides industry-like resources and funding for neurologic-related pharmaceutical development, from the stages of lead optimization up through phase I clinical trials. Likewise, the NCI has the *Developmental Therapeutics Program* (DTP), which funds all stages of pre-clinical development, and the *Cancer Therapy Evaluation Program* (CTEP) for clinical testing.

Biodefense is one emphasized combination area with many resources. Programs fund a combination of national security and health technologies, which may include everything from preventing flu outbreaks to antidotes for bioterrorism to medications for radiation leaks. Examples of funding sources include *Biomedical Advanced Research and Development Authority* (BARDA), which runs *Bioshield*, or the *Countermeasures Against Chemical Threats* (CounterACT) program. The DOD also sponsors the *Congressionally Directed Medical Research Program* (CDMRP), which funds research for a specific array of diseases that can be found on its website http://cdmrp.army.mil/.

Other programs, which do not include funding but which provide useful resources, include the *Molecular Libraries Program* http://mli.nih.gov/mli/, which provides small molecule libraries and high through-put screening, as well as the *National Disease Research Interchange* (NDRI), which provides a wide variety of human tissues, cells, organs, and biomaterials to researchers for a variety of endeavors, and also has useful genetic data and tissue banks: http://www.ndriresource.org/. These are just some of the examples that may provide ideas of how to take advantage of resources already available.

INVESTMENT CAPITAL

Often early stages of a company must be funded by the founders alone. These costs can vary significantly depending on the stage of the technology, intellectual property protection, prototype development, proof-of-concept studies, and other operational costs. Many founders of startup companies therefore spend much time seeking sources of funding, and in the process become quite accustomed to rejection. The most important stage of funding is arguably *seed funding*, when an idea is being built and tested. This seed funding may come in the form of grants discussed above, or incubators and accelerators discussed below, or from self-funding of the founders. Once an idea is shown to have promise, a startup company can typically begin attracting the interests of investors and financers.

Angel investors are those who seek to invest in very young companies and new ideas, whereas *venture capitalists* are more interested in expanding ideas and companies that have already proven themselves. Both angel investment groups and venture capital groups seek to invest in exchange for ownership in the company. Angel investors are much more willing, however, to invest in early stage technologies that hold the potential for later venture capital financing, and they are also more flexible in the types of companies in which they invest. Unlike many venture capital groups, angel investors usually invest their own money and usually have more motivation than simply seeing a large return on investment—they may want to help solve a particular problem, contribute mentorship, or be a part of the innovation in a particular field. Several tech companies, including Apple, Google, Facebook, and Yahoo (all registered trademarks) were made possible by some form of angel funding.

Bank loans, even when backed by the Small Business Administration (SBA), rarely provide financing to pre-revenue companies or companies with few assets, and therefore bank loans are not usually an option for early technology companies. Likewise, investment banks and venture capital groups generally do not invest in early stage, pre-revenue, pre-prototype companies, but each investment group is different, and venture capital groups tend to have specific criteria that they are looking for. Groups that are interested in technology firms are more likely to understand the up-front costs and development that are required before profitability.

Executive Summary

The first step for all business owners seeking capital is to write an executive summary. This is the bare minimum that will be required from any investor or lender. A more detailed report should also be made in a business plan, a template of which is provided in Appendix III. The executive summary itself essentially lays out the innovation of your product or service, a market analysis, and commercialization strategy. It should be no more than one page.

There are two general forms of an executive summary—one is to write it out in narrative (paragraph) form, and the other is to write it in a topical outline format (topic followed by a brief description, almost like question and answer). Either one is acceptable; each investor group may have a particular preference. More detailed descriptions of each component are described separately in subsequent sections of this section.

Either format of an executive summary should cover the topics shown in Table 6, with a brief description of each (not all components are required, but as many important details as possible should be included within the one page):

Table 6: Outline of an executive summary.

- Brief Summary (one sentence)
- Business Summary (primary business activities)
- Customer Problem (background)
- Customer Solution (products/services – description of the technology/innovation)
- Target Market/Customer
- Sales/Marketing Strategy
- Business Revenue Model
- Competitors
- Competitive Advantage/Value Proposition
- Intellectual Property
- Management Team (founders, managers, executives, and also advisors, attorneys, boards, prior investors, etc.)
- Financials
  - Current and Projected Revenues (list by actual year)

- Company Stage (pre- or post-revenue, conceptual, product in development, prototyping, product ready, or list amount of trailing 12 month revenue, etc.)
- Regulatory Issues
- Previous Capital/Investors
- Strategic Partners
- Pre-money Valuation (Initial, Current round)
- Capital Seeking
- Purpose of Capital
- Other Metrics (Employees, Contractors, Customers, Sales Numbers, etc.)

In addition to the executive summary, early on you should consider what your milestones are and how much money you will need to get through each milestone. Many components that are used to calculate funding needs and to project revenue and expenses. These details are not always included in a presentation itself, but are important for estimating and justifying funding requirements, and should be included in the more detailed business plan. The financial data should include projected expenses, such as capital expenditures, R&D expenses, material & supply costs, manufacturing expenses, facility costs, administrative expenses, staffing expenses, operating costs, intellectual property expenses, animal/human study expenses, regulatory approval expenses, and sales & distribution costs. Similarly, projected revenue may come from sales, licensing, consulting, grants, partnerships, or debt financing (although debt financing counts as both revenue and an expense or liability). A summary of projected earnings is almost always provided in an investor presentation. The investor presentation typically includes a summary broken down by year, with annual projections of gross revenue and net profit over the next 5-7 years.

It can seem intimidating to meet investors for the first time, but if you are prepared there is no reason to be nervous. Most investors are excited to hear a good pitch or new idea, and even if they are not interested in investing, they can usually offer sage advice and useful feedback, and they may know others who would be interested in your idea. You should not be ashamed of sacrifices you have made to bring your idea to fruition.

This following sections will help you understand how investments work, how investors think, what questions you will be asked, and how to best prepare an outstanding pitch.

Pitching to Investors

Pitching your ideas to potential investors can not only lead to funding, but also to great collaboration efforts and unexpected alliances. It is important to remember that investors are considering not just your technology, but the people they are investing in. It is essential to show them your expertise, dependability, ability to be flexible and adaptable, as well as the ability to be a leader, thinker, and innovator in your field. Although it is important to have people involved who can provide meaningful experience and expertise in order to inspire confidence in the investors, investors should also recognize that many successful innovators rose from no prior experience.

As you embark on this journey, do not be afraid to refine your idea, approach, or strategy, because everyone always has something to learn and improve on. If an investor does not show interest, it is acceptable to ask what deterred them or what they would like to have seen, but it is not wise to continue to try to persuade them.

You should be down to earth yet professional when presenting, and neither over-sell nor under-sell your idea. You should always lay out the problem that you are solving first. Many people jump right into discussing their idea or technology with insufficient background on the market problem or need they are addressing. Part of this is because pitches to investors are often very short, rarely more than 10-15 minutes, and innovators sometimes forget that even experts in closely-related fields may not be familiar with their technology or terminology, much less business professionals.

Nevertheless, venture capitalists are often people who have taken the initiative to educate themselves, and should be able to understand any business concept even if they don't understand exact mechanisms of the technology. In other words, if the investors do not understand your idea, you are not doing a good job explaining it. Venture capitalists are also becoming more educated in their understanding of technology and statistics, or at least hiring outside experts as consultants and for due diligence.

There are many conferences for presenting ideas to venture capitalists, usually organized by state or region. Most investor groups will only consider companies within their state or region, so it is best to seek these out first. You can also submit ideas directly to venture capital groups via their websites, but it is usually important to be introduced to the group through one of their colleagues; some investor groups only listen to pitches from trusted referrals and may not respond to unsolicited pitches. There is also an outstanding website www.gust.com where companies can summarize their ideas and submit it to multiple investor groups. This website connects angel and VC funds, often by the simple click of a button, rather than emailing an application to each group through their website. Some of the groups charge a fee to submit, mostly in order to filter out applications not specific to their group, but the majority allow free submission. The site also includes several types of alternative investment groups, including alumni organizations, incubators, and business development groups.

Naivety will be quickly exposed if unaware of competing technologies, competing companies, revenue model, or market data. It is amazing how many people do not even perform a simple internet search of competitors or related ideas. I have also seen where two companies presented nearly identical technologies at the same investor conference and did not know about each other, which was a little embarrassing for them. Therefore, the section on *Market Analysis & Strategy* will discuss important details that you should prepare for investors.

It may be a little excessive, but it is good preparation to not only know who your competition is, but to review details of their product line, future directions, and key financial data, before making a pitch to knowledgeable investors. This sort of data can be easily acquired if your competition is a public company—you can review their data just as you would if investing in their stock. Yahoo Finance, Google Finance, or any brokerage firm will list such data (e.g., look for "key statistics," "financials," "analyst coverage," etc., under the stock ticker of the competitor). Relevant data to your analysis and business plan may include market cap, revenue, cash flow, year over year growth, PEG ratio, profit & operating margin, return on equity, product line, primary competitors, and more.

You should be able to describe the important points of your technology without requiring non-disclosure agreements. You should describe in clear terms what the technology is without necessarily revealing confidential information. All details can be discussed one on one with interested parties and with appropriate agreements if necessary. Although it may be possible to steal an idea, usually the person behind the technology is just as important as the technology itself, perhaps due to expertise or vision or other less tangible factors. This was demonstrated in dramatic fashion with Steve Jobs and the rise and fall and rise of Apple. This applies even more in high-tech endeavors, where investors might have difficulty stealing ideas even if they had the opportunity. The best protection of course is simply to submit the appropriate patent applications and develop the IP as quickly as possible.

It is important to recognize that making the technology itself is not the endpoint—there are many difficult and risky steps after this. Other overarching points for a presentation include being transparent about the strengths and weaknesses of your position, technology, team, or market potential. This will establish credibility with the investors and show that you are well-educated in the field.

The last impression you make in the presentation should be a strong and compelling summary (essentially, a one-line pitch). This may include a re-emphasis of the impact, the competitive advantage, the market and earnings potential, or other unique aspects of your innovation.

Investors clearly are seeking to make profits in quite risky endeavors, and therefore they must consider not only the novelty of the idea, but the risks, timing, and potential in achieving a return on investment. Venture capitalists therefore seek to invest in companies with large market potentials (including some groups who only seek forecasts in the range of hundreds of millions of dollars). Investors also tend to stick to business industries and models with which they have experience. Naturally, investors also prefer proven and protected technologies, large markets with untapped potential, products with clear differentiating power, technologies with rapid growth potential, and business models with low burn rates and high cash flows.

The Presentation

Table 7 is a list of important points in a pitch to investors (basically following the executive summary). Keep in mind that presentations to investors should rarely be over 10-15 minutes, so some information will need to be brief or even left out. If investors are interested, they will ask more about the points that they want to know.

Table 7: Outline of an investor pitch.

- The Innovation
    - The problem or need
    - The solution
        - The technology and supporting evidence
        - The value proposition
        - The customer questions of "Why should I care?" and "Why should I believe you?"
        - Endorsements from preliminary customers or experts in the field
        - Stage of the technology (e.g., concept only, product in development, prototyping, product ready, etc.)
        - Other future applications and markets for the technology
- Market
    - Market Analysis & Strategy
    - Market size
    - Market growth, trends, and conditions
        - Anticipated evolution of the technology and field over time
    - Market acceptance/penetration and integration timeline (e.g., capture X% of the market in Y years)
    - Target Customer
    - Summary of these variables as expected revenue, profit, & growth over the next 5-7 years
        - Projected revenue = number of sales * price (annual basis)
        - Projected revenue = % market share * market size (annual basis)

- Business Model
  - Principle method of revenue
  - Estimated revenue, growth, & profit
    - Cash flow (e.g., annual revenue minus operating costs ≈ EBITDA)
    - Steps and milestones to achieve these projections
    - Time to profitability/Breakeven point
    - Expected profitability (e.g., profit percent = profit/revenue, based on market data above)
    - Time to exit
    - Operating costs/burn rate and ways to maximize revenue while minimize costs, etc.)
  - Commercialization considerations
    - Licensing
    - Salesforce
    - Distribution
    - Reimbursement
    - Competitive pricing analysis
    - Reimbursement strategy
    - Sustainability issues
- Competition
  - Your competitive advantage (could be the technology, the team, the approach, therapeutic advantage, buyer preferences, convenience, etc.)
  - Intellectual property protection
  - Risks (e.g., slow market adoption, competing technologies, failure of the technology, etc.)
- Milestones, Benchmarks, Timeline (particularly risk-lowering events)
  - Proof of concept studies
  - Prototype development timeline
  - Path to market (including major milestones and any clinical trials and regulatory hurdles)
  - Hiring needs
  - Equipment needs
  - Upscale manufacturing & supply chain management
  - Marketing and distribution
  - Costs associated with each of the above
  - Time to first sales

- - Time to profitability
- Exit Strategy
  - Strategy and Timeline (e.g., initial public offering (IPO), merger & acquisition (M&A), trade sale, etc.)
  - Financing – (series/phases/traunches)
    - Perhaps best to say, "We are seeking $X to achieve Y milestone in Z amount of time."
    - Previous capital already received (non-dilutive grants are especially impressive)
    - Purpose of the capital
    - Future anticipated funding phases and amounts
    - Anticipated partnerships and alliances
  - Personnel:
    - Corporate Leadership – e.g., CEO, COO, CFO, CSO, CTO, CMO, CLO, President, Vice-President, Founder, Principal, Head, Director, etc.
    - Board – Chair, Advisory Committee, Management, Directors, etc.
    - Attorneys, accounting firms, advisors, etc.

The following may also be included in the presentation (for example, in the opening and/or closing slide):

- Company name/motto
- Website
- Industry/field/operations
- Year founded
- Contact email/phone/address

A simple way of improving the look of the presentation is to put your company name with logo in the same position on each slide, e.g., in the corner of each slide. Logo transparency is most easily done with a PNG file pasted into PowerPoint, but other file types work well too (which can be made from Adobe Illustrator or Photoshop, or other software, see the *Graphic Design* section). This will give a distinguished look to the presentation and help investors remember your company.

Valuation

Valuation of a company's worth can be complex and has been described as more of an art than a science in young growing companies. It generally involves consideration of several variables, including potential value of intellectual property, market size, market share, management experience, projected earnings, financial standing, maturity, stage of any regulatory approvals, risk analysis, significance of the innovation, strength of the competitive advantage, valuation of comparable companies, and many other less tangible factors such as speed of market adoption or the potential for a successful exit. For more mature companies, cash flow and assets are a far more important factor in valuation. Early technology companies are more difficult to value because they may not yet have revenue or proof of concept, yet they can still hold tremendous potential. Thus even rigorous valuation protocols can both underestimate and overestimate the future potential valuation.

Pre-money valuation is the amount that you believe your company is worth before it receives any investment. This of course includes abstract factors in addition to the concrete, including future growth potential, financial projections, intellectual property, competitive advantage, and many other others. The reason that pre-money valuation matters at all is that it will essentially determine how percentage ownership is divided if someone invests in the company, as will be explained below. It is alright to not give a pre-money valuation of your company outright to potential investors, but you should have a range in mind. Interested investors can always present you with a term sheet, which will propose such terms and which is negotiable.

For pre-money valuation estimates, $1-10 million is probably a fair rough range for a small startup company that has shown some form of proof of concept, that has invested significant time, effort, and/or money to their technology, that has some technical advisors, and that has received some grant support from a reputable institution, and that has some form of intellectual property protection. If the idea has particularly high potential impact or has received significant grant funding and has strong support for success, the valuation may of course be more.

In general, you should determine a pre-money valuation (let's use $4 million as an example), added to the amount of funding you are seeking (let's use $2 million as an example). This suggests that you are seeking $2 million in exchange for a 50% stake in the company ($2 million/$4million), with a *post-money valuation* of $6 million. This 50% stake will usually be issued as preferred stock to the investors (as opposed to common stock). The first major investment by a venture capital group is called the series A round.

Later on, if the overall valuation of the company remains the same in a subsequent series B round of financing, then investors have neither lost nor earned value on their investment. If company valuation increases in subsequent financing rounds it is called an "up round," and if valuation decreases it is a "down round." For example, one might say, "Series B financing is anticipated to be up to $2 million and is expected to be an up round." To prevent potential losses on their stake in the company, especially when new shares are being offered, early investors will often use anti-dilution clauses to prevent their shares from being diluted or devalued.

There are many types of anti-dilution clauses, each of which has advantages and disadvantages for all parties involved. A common method is the broad-based weighted-average, where the conversion rate of the early investors' preferred shares to common shares is modified proportionally to the change in share valuation, thereby offsetting to some degree the loss in investment value.

So continuing the example from above, assume a series B investor is willing to invest an additional $2 million for a 29% stake in the company. This essentially sets the company valuation at $5 million in a series B round, down from the prior $6 million valuation (calculated from 29% = [$2,000,000]/[$2,000,000 + $5,000,000]). If there are 10 million total shares of stock in the company prior to the series B financing, then the series A preferred shares were originally worth $.60 each (presuming preferred shares originally had a 1:1 conversion to common stock). But the new valuation suggests a price of $.50 per share. The $2 million of new investment at $.50 per share would be the equivalent of 4 million new shares (=$2,000,000/$.50), but $2 million of new investment should have only equaled 3.33 million new shares at the original valuation of $.60 (=$2,000,000/.60). The broad-based weighted-average valuation is then calculated as ((10,000,000+4,000,000)/(10,000,000+3,333,333)) = 1.05. Thus each series A preferred share will now be convertible to 1.05 common shares after the series B financing rather than a 1:1 conversion.

Other anti-dilution provisions may be used, such as a narrow-based weighted-average or a full-ratchet. A full-ratchet is the strongest protection for early investors; in the example above, it would basically use the conversion of 1.2 for preferred to common shares, calculated from either 4,000,000/3,333,333 or $.60/$.50. In certain cases, an alternative method to anti-dilution is to create a stock option pool at the first round of investment in anticipation of issuing more shares. Shares can then be issued from this pool rather than causing dilution with issuance of new shares. (Stock option pools are actually commonly created as a tool for attracting skilled employees, allowing the company to pay stock rather than just cash.)

Clearly investment and equity provisions can quickly become complex. Added to this is the fact that investors often request liquidation preferences, warrants, deferred dividends, or other terms as part of their preferred shares, and this will usually also affect the price of remaining shares. It is important to note that anti-dilution provisions can sometimes deter future investors, so it is wise to retain an attorney who is familiar with these topics and can look out for you and your company's specific interests.

Nevertheless, do not worry too much about proposed deal terms from potential investors early on, since these can all be negotiated. It is more important to first focus on the innovation and creating potential for the company. Some potential investors may prefer proposals like, "We are seeking $X for Y valuation," but is not really necessary since it is all based on projected and negotiable numbers anyway. In reality, it is more important to know what funding needs you will have ($X) to reach important milestones, and if an investor wants to participate in your idea, then the investor should provide the appropriate resources to make the idea succeed, and ownership share can be negotiated.

If negotiating term sheets, you should take an active role in the process and ask lots of questions. Even with advisors and attorneys, you should be the intimately involved in all negotiations, terms, and contracts. The term sheet will generally lay out the proposed structure of company, financial agreements and obligations, and conditions of ownership in equity shares (e.g., liquidation rights, voting power, dividends, anti-dilution provisions, founder's shares, stock option pools, and other rules and protections).

Due diligence is conducted before investment in a company, as well as in cases of potential merger or acquisition. It is usually beneficial to have a non-disclosure agreement to prevent any public disclosure of important company details. Due diligence typically involves collection of documentation and detailed analysis of many aspects of the company, including legal business structure and operation, equity ownership and structure, personnel, compensation, licenses, permits, titles, intellectual property ownership and licensing, current contracts (e.g., collaborative contracts, licensing contracts, purchasing contracts, distribution contracts, worker contracts), financial records (e.g., accounting for all assets and liabilities, and including all accounting records and tax returns), any pending litigation, liens, or easements, as well as any other pertinent considerations. If a company is seeking to invest in another company, it will often also perform an accretive/dilutive analysis as part of the due diligence to determine how any merger or acquisition will affect the parent company's share value. After due diligence, the term sheet is negotiated.

The amount of ownership requested by investors will vary considerably based on many factors. The percentage ownership is based on balancing the amount of risk with the amount of funding needed. In essence, the farther along a company can get without dilutive financing, the higher the percentage of the company may be kept. In pre-revenue stages, investors will typically want majority ownership. For companies that need high upfront capital or must pass FDA regulatory approval, ownership of the founder is certainly below 50%, probably more in the 10-30% range or lower by the time all rounds of financing have been achieved. Also, some amount of shares should be kept with the company itself for use in subsequent stock offerings or for use as incentive to retain future executive management, senior staff, and other employees. Ownership of executives and senior staff is often in the single digits, but of course depends on the stage at which they begin working with the company and what terms they negotiated.

Use of Funds

Investors will want to know what you will use the money for and how it will help advance the company. As examples, it may be used to fill critical management, advance research and development, fund sales/marketing/distribution, expand facilities, obtain capital equipment, bridge grant funding, obtain intellectual property protection, complete regulatory requirements, retain regulatory consultants, or for many other purposes.

The operating costs mentioned above refer to expenses of facilities, administrative, equipment, staffing, materials, supplies, manufacturing, sales force, regulatory compliance, etc. In an investor presentation, you do not need to cover any of these details, but you may be asked about it at the time of due diligence.

It will be helpful if you can explain to investors what your milestones are, how you will achieve them, and how much funding you need for each phase. For example, a company may be seeking seed money to develop a prototype, series A financing to pursue regulatory approval, or series B financing to expand existing sales. The best description is a statement like, "We are seeking $X to achieve Y milestone in Z amount of time." Explaining the details and definitions of milestone achievement will instill confidence in the investors.

Often an investor group will provide funding on conditions of meeting certain milestones, thus offsetting risk for the investors, yet still providing enough capital to move forward. Other times early investors will put in the first round of funding (such as for prototype development or proof-of-concept), but leave later rounds of funding to other investor groups (such as for expansion of sales or regulatory approval processes).

Executive Management

In the early stages of a company, it is not extraordinarily unusual to exist as a virtual company, coordinated by email or periodic meetings for example. At this stage it is wise to make connections with many people who have experience in business development, exits, investments, leadership, and research success. This is because it will become important to put in place corporate leadership and management who instill confidence in the founders, researchers, and potential investors.

Venture capitalists tend to be closely involved in the companies they invest in, including detailed legal agreements, terms and conditions, as well as board representation, and therefore it is important that the investors have similar vision and goals as the founder(s) and that the investors provide skills and resources in addition to just money. For this reason, inasmuch as it is possible, strategic partnerships, collaborative alliances, and grants may be a better path towards developing the prototype of an innovative technology since the focus tends to be more on the technology itself rather than just a return on investment.

More than ever, investors want to take a much more active role in their investments, which is the right thing for them to do, but this may cause problems as not all investors are ideal leaders, knowledgeable experts, or valuable assets to the team. Therefore be careful of bringing people into ownership of the company just because they have money. This can prevent difficulties at later stages or during subsequent phases of funding.

Market Analysis & Strategy

Unfortunately, investors may not always be quite as excited about your technology as you are, but they will get very excited about a good market for a technology, especially if that market has the ideal characteristics of unanswered needs, significant size, and rapid growth. A market analysis should describe as many relevant variables as possible, such as market size, market growth, achievable market share, segments of the market, major and minor competitors, target customer, ease of adoption of the technology, target payer, pricing and margins, reimbursement issues, profitability and breakeven point, sales force, timelines for regulatory approvals, milestones or critical decision points, potential failure points, and future competing technologies (including those that may make the market itself obsolete), as well as any other aspects that might pertain to your particular technology. You should provide a graph of projected annual revenue and profit for the next 3-10 years (on the longer side if the technology will take longer to launch, e.g., 7-10 years for FDA regulated products).

Projected revenue can be estimated via several methods. The simplest method is to calculate the multiple of [estimated annual sales numbers] * [product price]. Sales numbers can be estimated from market size and market penetration. Similarly, projected revenue can be calculated as the multiple of [% market share] * [market size]. These projections of revenue, including their growth over time, should use realistic expectations that account for the time and cost of acquiring a certain market share. Also recognize that investors typically expect at least a 10-15x return on their investment.

When showing financial projections, it is common to use a vertical bar graph to show revenue forecasts by year. Next to each revenue bar, companies also often show either net profits or EBITDA ("earnings before interest, taxes, depreciation, and amortization," which is simply like an earnings statement before any payment of taxes, interest, depreciation, or amortization).

Revenue projections may be based on a variety of data and technical analysis, but in the end it is all still just an educated guess. Just be sure that you can justify your projections in some regard, even if others might not agree with them. It is alright to have a big vision, but in order to gain the respect of investors it should be somewhat tempered by realistic assumptions, or even better, by using an independent market analysis. Using independent sources to verify market data and to develop a solid market strategy is important when seeking funding.

Many technical market research reports are available for a variety of industries, fields, and products. These can be expensive, often costing hundreds or even thousands of dollars per report, but they are very detailed and are one of the best ways to validate your market potential to investor groups. Some examples of market report resources are http://www.emarketer.com/, http://www.marketreports.com/, http://www.marketresearch.com/, and http://www.mintel.com/. For those associated with academic centers, these reports can often be found for free, such as through an institution's or business school's library journal access (which likely includes access to at least one of the websites above).

In addition, the National Institute of Standards and Technologies (NIST) has created the National Innovation Marketplace (NIM), a collaborative effort where inventors, manufactures, and venture capitalists can team up on projects and where innovative technologies can receive their own market analysis. The website can be found at http://innovationsupplychain.com/. This tool can provide independent comprehensive analysis of your technology or idea, rate its market potential, and can even post and advertise your technology and compare it to others in the field, where manufacturers, collaborators, and investors may contact you for more information. It also allows companies to request or provide professional and technical services. To post your technology or idea, go to http://innovationsupplychain.com/post.php. Other independent market analysis reports for your particular product or service may offered by a variety of consulting services, but naturally this is much more expensive than general market analysis reports.

All business is continually evolving and adapting, and business plans and strategies should change accordingly. In fact, businesses rise and fall on the ability to stay a step ahead of current technology. You will need to continually adjust your approach and hypothesis to the customer problem, the technology solution, the distribution and pricing strategy, the marketing and sales strategy, and product proof-of-concept both from a scientific perspective and from a business perspective.

Therefore, try to think ahead about how competitive your idea really is… is your innovation protectable (with patents, trade secrets, or unique branding or services, etc.)? Can others copy the product, service, or model, and if so, is your idea adaptable to future fluxes and advances in the field? If it is a medical product, would it require doctors to change their practice, and if so, would it be an inconvenience, or would it establish a new standard of care that doctors would seek to adopt? Is the market crowded with other technologies that may be different but that target the same indications? Are you claiming that your technology targets a broad condition when in reality it only targets a small subset of that condition? Does the technology shift current demand from one product to another, or does it create a whole new market and demand, or perhaps serve as a platform technology for other innovations? Would the product launch be into one particular segment of the market (as a "beachhead launch") and then expand as a platform technology for other markets?

Another important consideration that is familiar to engineers but often overlooked by others is the ability to upscale manufacturing and create efficient supply chains. For example, a medical technology could be very effective for individual patients, but if it is difficult to upscale this can cause major cost and supply problems. One example of this includes recent regenerative medicine efforts using autologous stem cells, which, although potentially revolutionary, requires extracting certain tissues or cells from the patient, modifying genetics or structure or function, and then restoring the tissues or cells to the patient. The time and labor involved with each patient, combined with reimbursement issues, create significant barriers to this technology (not to mention tighter regulations as the FDA becomes stricter on purported stem cell regenerative therapies that have unknown risks and surreptitious efficacy). Clearly, good ideas can still suffer due to relatively simple logistical problems in business.

Commercialization

A commercialization plan begins by answering the most basic questions that a business executive or investor would want to know: What problem does your innovation address? Who is the customer or beneficiary? How is your benefit unique? What makes your technology more likely to succeed? The company's survival is dependent on the unique value that it provides to a customer, i.e., the value proposition. This value to the customer may exist in any number of factors, e.g., the uniqueness or novelty of the product, the perceived value, the convenience and efficiency, the quality and reliability, or the price. Table 8 shows a simple outline of a commercialization plan.

Table 8: Outline of a commercialization plan.

- Value proposition of the technology
- Expected impact and outcomes
- Expected customers and cost analysis
- Vision and goals of the company (milestones, growth, expected achievements, etc.)
- Current state of the company (size, sales, funding, achievements, experience, management, technology, regulatory approvals, etc.)

- Marketing (size, growth, target customer, achievable share, expected hurdles, regulatory approvals, competition, what makes your product unique, strategic alliances, licensing agreements, marketing plans, distribution methods, direct sales, resellers, sales force, staffing, etc.)
- Strategy for intellectual property protection (patent, trade secret, licensing, regulatory protections, etc.)
- Financing plan (describe the source and amount of funding, steps you will take to obtain funding, or conditional letter of intent or commitment for funding, etc.)
- Plan for production and manufacturing (in-house or contracted manufacturing, etc.)
- Plan for sales and distribution (in-house, contracted, or via partners/collaboration, etc.)
- Revenue and profit projections (sources of revenue, sustainability, known and unknown factors, etc.)

The commercialization plan is essential to phase II and III of SBIR/STTR grants, and it should address all the above questions. This may also include discussion of everything in the business plan and investor presentation, described previously (e.g., market size, market growth, target customer, achievable market share, competitors and competitive analysis, positioning, sales projections, pricing and margin analysis, strategic partnerships/mergers/acquisitions, licensing agreements, marketing strategy, and milestones). Risks should also be addressed, including scientific barriers, intellectual property issues, technical challenges, risk of market adoption, scale-up and manufacturing issues, reimbursement expectations and challenges, and other financial risks. For SBIR/STTR commercialization plans, grant reviewers also prefer to see that companies will have financial support of investors or banks should they need it.

As mentioned previously, market research reports are essential to a good commercialization plan. Many technical market research reports are available for variety of industries, fields, and products to validate a market potential and market approach, as well as the commercial feasibility of the business venture.

Marketing

Marketing itself is something that may be overlooked by the scientifically minded. It is easy to believe that a product will sell itself simply because it is superior to other products. This may be true in some cases, but marketing and branding can be essential to a successful company. Certainly this does not mean vapid or obnoxious advertising that many marketing firms promote (and that even many experts now doubt to be effective, particularly in today's saturated environment). Rather, creating an atmosphere along the lines of novelty or even exclusivity can be very successful, as Apple, Google, Facebook, and others have shown. Many technologies do not need vacuous infomercial-type marketing, but rather intelligent marketing and brand identity that appeal to and impress a more fastidious audience, thereby retaining a strong customer base.

The image for your company and brand will depend heavily on your website and web presence. Although there are many ways to make a website quite elaborate, it is often best to stick with a very simple yet well-designed website. Adding videos, interactive animations, sounds, or other accessories can actually deter website traffic and make it difficult for people with certain operating systems, mobile access, or slow connection speeds to have unimpeded access to your site. It is also worth reviewing the section on *Search Engine Optimization*, emphasizing the importance of internet presence, social media, and press coverage.

The list of marketing avenues is nearly endless; today's opportunities range from social media and internet campaigns to more traditional radio and television outlets and local sponsorships. With some creativity, a company can find the right medium for their service or product, achieving both effective and cost-efficient methods of advertising, thereby accelerating market adoption of new technology.

Sales may be accomplished via several routes, for example, through the company itself, through a partner company, or through a contracted sales force. If possible, a combination of these methods may be beneficial to a small company, so that if one method falls through, the company has already prepared a separate pathway for success. Forming contracts or partnerships specifically for sales and distribution can rapidly increase sales revenue, particularly when customers may need to be trained or informed about a technology before they will adapt to using it. When forming such alliances, beware of conflicts of interest with other sales products or of lack of ability to complete the proposed work. This is typically protected by cancellation rights and alteration clauses in an agreement.

Exit Strategy

An exit strategy is a strategy for investors to obtain a return on their investment while also turning over responsibility and liability for the company to another party. Even though company revenue is an incentive for shareholders to stay in the company, great profits can often (but not always) be made by a strategic exit. The most common exit strategies are either an initial offering of public stock (IPO), a merger with or acquisition by another company (M&A), or for certain companies, an outright sale of the company to a private buyer. The most advantageous exit strategy depends on many factors, including many factors within the industry and the market conditions of the time.

If planning on an M&A exit strategy, it is important to know who potential acquirers would be and to model your company and products in a way that makes the acquisition attractive to the purchasing company. It may be advantageous to form such alliances early, but not if technology could be stolen, copied, or independently developed.

Market conditions for IPOs, and particularly interests in various high-tech industries, wax and wane considerably over the years. In addition to market timing, the company must gauge what milestones it can achieve to maximize value in the company and not sell itself short of its potential. Interestingly, because market conditions vary significantly, IPOs may sometimes actually provide less predictable and less substantial return on investment compared to merger or acquisition. Thus IPOs are sometimes postponed or cancelled when investor interest is below expectations. On the other hand, sometimes preparing a company for an IPO will reciprocally catalyze the interests of potential buyers.

Regarding IPOs, stock markets often attribute value for growth companies somewhere around 10-30 times annual earnings (PE ratio of 10-30). For some young companies, PE ratio may be much greater, or may even be infinite ("undefined PE ratio") since many unprofitable companies technically have share value even without profits. Thus many other measures are also used to determine an appropriate price for public shares of a company, but in reality, stock price tends to be determined more by demand and timing than by concrete valuation measures.

Importantly, becoming a publicly traded company puts many obligations on a company to make disclosures of finances and important milestones, and also makes the company susceptible to hostile takeovers, where others may purchase majority ownership of shares despite the wishes of the company.

Congress is currently seeking to make it easier for small companies to offer IPOs. The management and accounting of public companies is regulated by the Sarbanes-Oxley Act, but new pending legislation (the JOBS Act) could allow smaller companies an easier path to IPO by limiting the requirements for outside, independent accounting controls and audits, and it could simultaneously ease the obligation for certain private companies to go public (such as those with over a certain amount of invested capital or over a certain number of investors—see the Investment Regulations section for more information).

Many other variations of exit strategies also exist. For example, a reverse takeover is an alternative method of taking a private company public. Instead of offering public shares through an IPO, which can be a formidable undertaking, this strategy acquires the shares of a pre-existing public corporation (which may or may not be currently operational), and merges the two companies so that the private company is now public.

Of note, even after a company is publicly traded, it can raise further capital by making secondary stock offerings. This method works by selling remaining shares owned by the company, or by diluting shares of current share owners. The disadvantage is that this diminishes the value of the shares and/or ownership of the company.

Another similar method of raising further capital after already existing as a publicly traded company is to offer shares to a specific private investor (or investor group, hedge fund, mutual fund, etc.)—this is called a P.I.P.E. for "private investment in public equity." This also has the disadvantage of possibly diluting current share value and deterring public confidence in the stock, but the private investor benefits from purchasing a significant portion of the company, usually for a price less than would be obtainable on the public market or with special conditions that guarantee the sale of the shares for a special price (e.g., preferred shares), and the company likewise benefits from a direct infusion of cash and less burdensome regulations than a secondary offering. Yet another similar method consists of offering preferred shares that pay some form of interest (cash, equity, warrants to purchase more equity, etc.) in addition to the typical benefits of preferred shares (this is often called mezzanine financing).

Investment Regulations

It should be noted that if you intend to solicit money or property from other persons to finance the operation of your business, you may need to first file certain information with the State Commission's Division of Securities (DOS) or State Corporation Commission (SCC), as well as with the Securities and Exchange Commission (SEC). These regulatory agencies typically govern money managers, brokerage firms, financial institutions, investment banks, etc., but also cover companies that raise capital through equity, bonds, notes, cash deposits, etc. Fortunately, many startup companies can present their business pitch to registered investor groups prior to registering themselves under various exemptions that exist for small companies, but it is wise to review the state laws and codes to be sure you are in compliance, especially before actually receiving any investment funding.

SEC exemptions for companies seeking funding for equity can be found under Regulation D (see rules 504, 505, & 506). The business owner(s) can often seek investment capital without registration as long as they are not receiving a commission for the offering, as long as it is a small private business, as long as the investment opportunity is not advertised to the public, as long as the investors are accredited investors, and/or as long as the investors are made aware that the offering is considered to be *restricted securities* (meaning there are SEC limitations on when and to whom the equity can be sold). The sale of equity to private investors is sometimes classified as a *private placement*, which is often done under the legal agreement of a private placement memorandum (PPM). The PPM details the terms of the offering and all potential risks involved.

Beware "finders," "consultants," "brokers," and others who claim to help you obtain funding. You should not hire people to solicit investments. Not only do most reputable VC's look down on this, but it also may be illegal under your state's Division of Securities.

Misrepresenting company information and material can be illegal, even if done unknowingly. This material can include the description of your business and its operations, financial documents, capitalization methods and strategy, use of the investor's money, description of securities being offered and pertinent rights and limitations, the details of the offering (including how much is being offered and who is being compensated), risk factors for your business and industry, financial disclosures including credit history, compensations, transactions, criminal violations, taxation aspects, previous offerings and/or principal shareholders, or any lawsuits or other current complicating factors involving the company.

Offering equity positions to raise capital can be complex, and is therefore an area where it is helpful and important to have legal counsel to protect your interests. As discussed previously, there are not only many potential pitfalls, but also legal regulations surrounding these undertakings.

As a side note, the JOBS Act (currently pending at the time of this publishing with bipartisan support despite some controversy) intends to allow new advantages for small businesses who wish to raise funding and go public, including temporary exemption from the SEC requirements for accounting and auditing controls. It would also raise the threshold for obligatory SEC registration of a private company from $5 million to $50 million in investment funding and from 500 to 1,000 in total number of investors. It also intends to lift regulations that would have otherwise inhibited small companies from seeking crowd-funding (see the section on *Other Financing Methods*).

Incubators & Accelerators

Other valuable resources are also available to startup companies, including startup incubators and accelerators. Several incubator organizations exist, but vary tremendously in the type and quality of services they offer. Some of them simple provide connections to business professionals and mentorship, some ask for a percentage of the company, some provide office space and equipment, some cater only to certain industries. Appendix VII lists many incubator and accelerator resources for startup tech companies. Local public and private institutions may also be able to provide some guidance as part of economic development initiatives.

Other Financing Methods

An important form of funding that is often overlooked is collaborative agreements or partnerships with other companies, foundations, or institutions that might have an interest in certain work. Many larger companies are willing to fund R&D through small business channels, and in return will often ask for either exclusive licensing to the technology or equity ownership in the company. This may have the added benefit of taking pressure off of later sales and distribution efforts, but can complicate exit strategies and ownership of intellectual property. With some creativity and networking, you may be able forge joint ventures or partnerships for research purposes, or find state financing programs, research contracts, crowd-funding, or other federally-sponsored or industry-sponsored research and production programs. Partnerships in particular may be beneficial because of the ability to share resources and expertise that may be out of reach for an individual startup company. A partnership may take any form of licensing agreement, product development contract, sales agreement, or even equity investment. Therefore, as with investors, it is important that two partnering firms share similar vision and goals.

There are other considerations for university developed technologies. For example, the investigator and university must consider whether licensing is a better idea than forming a company, and the investigator must also consider whether the university will even be cooperative with a spinoff company even if it is in their best interest. Therefore, when developing a technology out of university support, it is important to first discuss your intent with the university's tech-transfer or tech-management office (especially before applying for an STTR grant).

Nevertheless, academically supported researchers have many available options for funding (including technology commercialization grants, virtual incubator grants, microgrants, R21 and R01 grants, or other university based support and collaborative grants). Of note, R01 and R21 grants can also go to small businesses conducting exploratory or basic science research, but due to the competitive advantages and vast pool of academically and institutionally supported researchers, these can be difficult to obtain and are likely to provide less funding than SBIR/STTR.

Crowd-funding is another new method to fund startup ideas (e.g., sites like www.microryza.com, www.kickstarter.com, or www.indiegogo.com). Funding is pooled from a variety of interested persons, sometimes solely out of individual interest, or sometimes in return for sponsorship, or less often as a loan or equity position in the idea. As discussed, the JOBS Act allows more leniency for small businesses to advertise for and receive crowd-funding from many small investors (which might otherwise fall under SEC regulations—see *Investment Regulations*).

Another resource is to join societies and organizations associated with your endeavor. These can easily be found on LinkedIn or with simple keyword internet searches. These might include associations and councils in technology, engineering, medical devices, biotechnology, healthcare, and/or science subspecialties.

Other "business development services" are often available in local communities and states, financed by federal, state, or local economic development funds, but these often only provide advice or networking and often even charge fees. They will often describe some sort of array of grants or loans that your company is missing out on, but these services generally seem vague and not particularly helpful.

If you already have a product that the government might be interested in, many government contracts are available. There are *bid* and *non-bid* type contracts, meaning that the conditions of the purchase are either on the government's terms or your terms, respectively. Non-bid contracts are available through the DOD (e-procurement) or through the *General Services Administration* (GSA). In addition to federal purchasing, there are also many state, city, and educational purchasing systems. By becoming a GSA contractor and obtaining a GSA schedule you allow the government, perhaps the largest purchaser in the world, to have direct purchase power through your business. When you register through CCR.gov or SAM.gov (e.g., as mentioned under the *SBIR/STTR Grants* section), you will likely also receive solicitations for assistance with obtaining these government contracts.

Similarly, if you already have a product that you can produce (i.e., little to no R&D needed), the government and many private companies will contract their needs using requests for quotation (RFQ) or requests for proposal (RFP) to supply certain needs of a purchaser. This is especially common for engineering companies, such as a defense contractor who subcontracts various aspects of a project to smaller companies. Also, an indefinite delivery/indefinite quantity (IDIQ) contract is like a GSA contract that is often used for engineering or architectural services. In these cases, the larger company may choose to do a quality audit of the smaller company to ensure quality and consistency of the products and services.

For more mature companies that have revenue, *corporate bonds* (or *commercial paper notes* for short-term offerings) may be another method of financing. These function essentially the same as government bonds, where an investor purchases a promissory note that allows redemption of the bond for a certain price, and interest is paid to the investor at some predetermined rate based on the original price of the bond (usually $1000). Alternatively a *convertible bond*, allows conversion to shares rather than cash redemption, typically at a pre-determined discounted rate. Corporate bonds, like an IPO, are done through an underwriter, typically an investment bank or group of banks.

§

PART III – INTELLECTUAL PROPERTY

"I am sure of nothing, and find myself having to say
'I don't know' very often. After all, I was born not knowing
and have only had a little time to change that here and there.
It is fun to find things you thought you knew, and then to discover
you didn't really understand it after all."
Richard Feynman, *Letter to Armando Garcia J 1985*

"I am enough of an artist to draw freely upon my imagination.
Imagination is more important than knowledge."
Albert Einstein, *Interview 1929*

"I have no special talents. I am only passionately curious."
Albert Einstein, *Letter to Carl Seelig 1952*

There are many types of intellectual property, including utility patents, design patents, trademarks, copyrights, and trade secrets. Each plays an important and specific role. For applications to the U.S. Patent and Trademark Office (USPTO), it is very beneficial to obtain an EFS-web account because it will allow fast and easy submission of patent applications and supporting documentation. Instructions are found here: http://www.uspto.gov/patents/process/file/efs/guidance/register.jsp. It takes a couple weeks to be authenticated as a registered EFS-web user and to receive a customer number and digital certificate file required for login. New applications can be registered on the eFile system, and all submitted documentation and USPTO communication can be viewed on the PAIR system. Both systems can be found at the USPTO Electronic Business Center: http://www.uspto.gov/patents/ebc/index.jsp.

Trademark

A trademark is a protected mark that corresponds to a specific product or service. It may include a logo, symbol, image, word, phrase, or combination of these. It can provide indefinite protection as long as certain conditions are met, and it protects brands, products, services, etc. The application can be done online in a matter of minutes, but it is also important to make sure the mark has not already been claimed. A simple search on the *Trademark Electronic Search System* (TESS) and *Trademark Application and Registration Retrieval System* (TARR) of the USPTO, as well as a general internet search, will reveal whether you have a good chance of having a unique mark that will be allowed as trademark. Marks that are in common use or merely common descriptive terms for products or services will likely not qualify for trademark protection.

Once you have a unique idea in mind, you must first decide whether to submit the trademark as simple letters/words, or whether it involves the use of a specific image, design, or logo, either with or without words. An application for the word or phrase itself provides the broadest protection. Secondly you must decide what category of product or service your trademark relates to. The various categories are listed as selectable options in the online trademark application with the USPTO. The final cost is based on the number of categories to which you claim that your trademark applies. Many subcategories are listed within each category, and the number of subcategories selected does not increase the cost. Lastly, you must claim whether the mark is already used in commerce or whether you intend to use the mark in commerce in the future. The trademark can be filed online at http://www.uspto.gov/teas/e-TEAS/index.html and costs $275 if filing in a single category. You should consider filing a trademark for your company name and for any products or services that you will offer. A servicemark is the same as a trademark, but used for services rather than tangible products.

If the mark is already in common use or would be likely to cause confusion or overlap with generally used terms, phrases, or images, it is unlikely to be granted. Similarly, if the mark is simply descriptive or similar to other marks already protected by trademark, it will likely not be granted. Before final registration of the trademark, you may use the ™ symbol to show trademark protection is in process. After several months, if there are no objections or concerns from the USPTO, the mark will be published publicly for any opposition, and the trademark office will likely ask for evidence of use of the mark in commerce and allow a timeframe for this to be accomplished. If there are objections, these may fall under standard objections that can easily be addressed with the assistance of a trademark attorney.

If the USPTO has no further objections, the mark may obtain registered status, and the ® symbol should then be used. Protection of the mark is best maintained by market use, but without making the mark become the common product/service itself; in other words, the trademark should generally be used as an adjective or brand for the category of product or service, not as the product/service itself, because this can diminish the likelihood of long-term trademark protection.

The USPTO lists the common reasons for trademark rejection to be confusion with other marks, merely descriptive or generic terms, merely a surname, deceptive or misdescriptive marks, multiple marks in one application, use of an already protected symbol, or use in a manner that does not fit the purpose of a trademark.

Design Patent

A design patent is similar to a trademark but protects the unique design of a product in an artistic or ornamental sense, not in the novelty sense of a utility patent. Examples could include the design of electronic gadgets, medical devices, stylized accessories, or even desktop icons. No innovative or functional aspect of the product is protected, only the visual design.

Copyright

A copyright is granted to any "original works of authorship," including works or expressions of ideas, but it does not protect the conceptual ideas themselves or methods of using the ideas. Rather, it protects the form of expression, such as the writing of a book, the performance of a musical piece, the performance of a play, or the displaying of a work of art, thereby excluding others from using or distributing such work. The copyright exists from the moment the work is created, but in the case of unpublished works the time of creation of the work must verifiable. The copyrighted work may be registered at the U.S. Copyright Office (and also deposited with the Library of Congress with a control number if it is a published work that libraries might acquire). The copyrighted work should state the owner's name and the year in which it was copyrighted with the © symbol. The author (and sometimes the employer of the author) is considered the owner of the copyright unless other legal agreements are made. A copyright generally lasts 70 years after the author's death, or in the case of contracted or anonymous works, 95 years after first publication or 120 years after original creation, whichever is shorter.

Trade Secret

An idea, invention, or process that is not likely patentable, or which would be difficult to protect with a patent, is often best kept as a trade secret, since submitting the details required in a patent application would release the intellectual property to the public. A trade secret is recognizable in court if reasonable efforts have been made to protect the trade secret and the trade secret was illegitimately exposed, but trade secrets do not have much recourse once they become public (although the Economic Espionage Act and the Computer Fraud Abuse Act may provide some legal protections).

Utility Patent

A utility patent, as opposed to a design patent, does not protect any artistic design, but protects the novel function or utility of an invention. Therefore, a utility patent is one of the most important types of intellectual property protection to a technology company. Whether an idea or invention is patentable is not always clear up front, but in general, it must be novel, useful, and not obvious, and it must be "patentable subject matter," which essentially includes four categories: "any new and useful *process, machine, manufacture,* or *composition of matter,* or any new and useful improvement thereof, may obtain a patent therefor," according to the U.S. patent office (35 U.S.C. 101, italics added). The patent office does not allow patents on "laws of nature, natural phenomena, or abstract ideas." Interestingly, however, patents on genes, polypeptides, and enzymes are allowable, but these sorts of patents usually need to include a functional claim of use (e.g., methods of using the product to treat a disease), an alteration to the natural product (e.g., a recombinant form of the gene), or a process of isolation or purification (e.g., using cell lines to express the gene or protein).

A patent application must be submitted in each country where you hope to achieve patent protection. You cannot usually obtain a patent in one country alone and then later file in other countries, since patent applications must be filed within a certain amount of time of first publication or within a certain amount of time of the claimed priority date of the first patent application. In other words, you must file a foreign application usually somewhere between 3 months and 1 year of the original patent submission, depending on the country.

Some regional systems allow an application to be submitted to a group of countries, such as the European Patent Office (EPO), or the Patent Cooperation Treaty (PCT), which is sometimes called an "international patent," but is not actually an international patent system per se but rather a system of submitting a patent application to the many individual countries under the PCT, including the US, the EPO, and many others. This provides a priority date for the application that is recognized by all countries under the PCT. Any idea that was published publicly before filing the patent application risks dismissal of the patent as public domain (in the U.S., public disclosure of the idea may be allowed up to one year before the patent application, but this is not usually allowed in other countries).

The time and expense required for filing a patent are significant but can clearly offer great rewards. Larger companies have a significant advantage in this regard, including money and legal expertise. Going at it alone could theoretically be done for quite cheap, with application and maintenance fees in the U.S. adding up to a bare minimum of $5755 over the life of the patent (see Table 9). Using legal assistance to file and maintain patents in every major country, however, can quickly approach a million dollars or more. Naturally the country that tends to offer the most financial incentive for the work involved is the United States. Also of note, there may be some advantages to first filing a PCT application as a means for filing in the U.S. as well as in other countries, but this depends on certain factors and it is wise to consult an attorney for this strategy.

Table 9: Minimum USPTO utility patent fees for small entities.

Filing Fee (electronic)	$95
Examination Fee	$125
Search Fee	$310
Issuance Fee	$870
Maintenance Fee (Year 3.5)	$565
Maintenance Fee (Year 7.5)	$1425
Maintenance Fee (Year 11.5)	$2365

A *provisional patent* is an extremely useful and inexpensive tool that allows you to submit your invention in an informal manner a year in advance of filing the formal utility patent application. The provisional manuscript does not need to follow the formal rules that a utility patent does, but should include names of the inventor(s), complete description of the invention, how to make use of the invention, relevant prior art and improvement over existing technology, etc. You then have exactly one year (not a day longer) to submit the official *non-provisional* utility patent application. The non-provisional patent can then later address the above aspects in more detail as well as protect against ways that others might try to design around the patent.

The provisional filing assigns an application number and sets a priority date, protecting your idea early on while giving extra time to assemble a formal application. The provisional patent is not actually reviewed by the patent office when determining whether the non-provisional patent will be granted, nor is it combined or published with the formal patent application. If you choose to abandon the application, no action needs to be taken, the provisional application simply expires. When filing the formal non-provisional application, be sure to claim priority of the provisional application by referencing the provisional application number in the Application Data Sheet under "Domestic Benefit/National Stage Information."

After submission of the patent application, the patent office reviews the application and notifies the inventor if any formatting needs to be fixed or if any additional parts need to be submitted. The office then assigns a group and class depending on the subject of the patent (the "art unit"), and the examining attorney reviews the general application to make sure everything is in order.

The patent application is published to the public about 18 months after submission unless a request is made for no publication (which can only be done if not filing in other countries). At about 24 months the examining attorney provides a response ("office action"), which may reject some or all of the claims and describe why the objections are made. The inventor is then given a chance to amend the claims or to present arguments to the examiner's objections justifying why the claims should in fact be allowed. The examiner then decides whether to accept or reject the amendments or arguments.

If more than one invention is claimed in the patent, the office will notify the inventor that only one invention may be selected for review. If that one invention is granted patent protection, the other claimed inventions can later optionally be re-incorporated into the patent as dependent claims on the first invention. As an example, if you invent a device, and also include claims for a method of making the device and a method of using the device, the patent office only allows you to select one of the three as the primary invention—for example, choosing the device as the primary invention—and then if the patent is granted, a request may be made for re-incorporation and examination of the other two types of method claims as dependent on the original device claims. Alternatively, you could also submit the two types of method claims above as divisional applications (see below), or, if strong enough to stand on their own, they can be submitted separately as independent utility patent applications.

When possible, filing multiple features of an invention as separate utility applications reinforces the protective strength of the patents, particularly in case of any patent challenges, since at least one of the features is likely to stand and since the cost to challenge each patent is immense. However, sometimes individual features or methods involved in an invention are not patentable by themselves, since they may have been covered in prior art or by themselves do not meet criteria for patentability. In other words, the invention must have at least one stand-alone feature that meets patentability criteria, but may have additional features added on that have been covered in prior art, as long as such features are predicated ("dependent") on the novel feature or aspect of the invention.

If the patent is allowed, the inventor pays an issuance fee; if the patent is rejected, the inventor may abandon the application, further amend the application and request reconsideration, request *continued examination*, or file a new application. If there are valid arguments against an examiner's rejection, the inventor may also appeal to the Board of Patent Appeals and Interferences.

A *continuing application* is different from a request for *continued examination*. A continuing application is filed as a continuation of a previously filed patent, with the purpose of seeking further applications and protections for the original invention. A continuing application has different subtypes: a *divisional* application claims a sort of distinct sub-invention out of the inventor's original invention, while a *continuation-in-part* maintains much of the original subject matter but also adds new information to the inventor's original patent.

The time from filing a patent application to allowance of the patent takes about 3-5 years, but can vary depending on the class of the technology and the number of arguments and modifications made. Patent protection expires 20 years after the initial filing date if maintenance fees are paid at four year intervals.

Once a patent is issued, the inventor may request *reissue* if errors are found that need to be updated or corrected. Sometimes this avenue is used to broaden the claims of the original patent, but it cannot be used beyond two years from the patent issue date, nor can it be used to add new narrowing or dependent claims. As opposed to a reissue, a *reexamination* can be requested by anyone for the purposed of raising a concern about the patentability of any claim in a patent, and this process is often used to challenge the patent itself rather than requesting a declaratory judgment procedure or enduring the risk of infringement claims.

It should be noted that when conducting research that may utilize other patented material, such utilization is not typically considered to legally infringe on the patent as long as the work is not being used to generate revenue. This exemption is called the "experimental use privilege," and allows basic research and development to continue using patented material, but typically does not allow commercialization to begin in anticipation of a patent expiring. In the case of diagnostics and devices, this generally means that FDA clinical trials cannot begin if another's patent is still in force and has not yet expired. However, in the case of drugs, the Hatch-Waxman Act not only allows R&D on patented agents, but also allows commercial manufacturing and clinical testing all the way through FDA approval even while another's patent is still in force. This allows, for example, generic drugs to hit the market by the time a drug patent expires.

Of note, a pharmaceutical agent may also be protected with methods apart from a utility patent itself. These methods include market exclusivity granted by legislative acts (such as the 5-year maximum extension of market exclusivity provided by the Hatch-Waxman Act), or in certain cases of new trials conducted for pediatric patients (1 year) or for obtaining over-the-counter (OTC) status (up to 3 years). Drugs can also remain competitive after patent by applying for new drug indications or by reformulating the drug.

A special type of patent is the plant patent, which is essentially a utility patent with special conditions. This allows patent protection on plant species that are created by human intervention (not nature) and that have been reproduced asexually (not including tubers). More detailed explanations can be found on the USPTO website: http://www.uspto.gov/web/offices/pac/plant/

Software presents a unique and unresolved situation, because in many cases it is not patentable, and although it can be copyrighted, a copyright is not adequate to protect against variations in similar software code that can serve identical functions (remember that a copyright simply protects the literal expression of an author, but not an idea, subject, or invention). Therefore software is usually kept unpublished as a trade secret (and unpublished works can qualify for copyright protection). Processes and methods can be patentable, but typically must meet the qualifications under the "machine-or-transformation test," which states that the process or method must either be performed by a machine specifically for that purpose, or must transform something from one state to another. Processes and methods outside these criteria are much less likely to be patentable, but some bounds of these criteria still remain unclear in current patent law.

It is wise for a company to periodically review its intellectual property and assess whether technologies have been developed and refined in ways that warrant updating patent protection, including whether it would be cost efficient to do so. Innovative entrepreneurs should also think ahead to future technologies related to their field and prepare to file these patents before others do.

Writing the Patent

A utility patent application should generally include the elements listed in Table 10. Each bulleted section should be on a separate page. The order does not really matter since each part is labeled and submitted electronically as a separate file. The format should use at least 1.5 line spacing, 1" margins, and embedded fonts in PDF files (which can be created from Word documents by saving as a PDF or printing from Word to Adobe PDF or PrimoPDF software).

Table 10: Outline of a utility patent application.
- *Title of Invention, Inventor(s)*
- *Abstract*
- *Specifications*
  - *Background of the Invention*
  - *Brief Summary of the Invention*
  - *Detailed Description of the Invention*
  - *Description of Preferred Embodiments*
  - *Brief Description of the Drawings (if applicable)*
  - *Detailed Description of the Drawings (if applicable)*
  - *Glossary of Terms and Abbreviations (if applicable)*
  - *Biosequence Listing (if applicable)*
  - *Chemical or Mathematical Formulae (if applicable)*
  - *Statement of Federally Sponsored Research (if applicable)*
- *Claims*
- *Drawings*
- *References (IDS – Form SB08)*
  - *References to Related U.S. Patents*
  - *References to U.S. Patent Applications*
  - *References to Foreign Patents*
  - *References to Non-Patent Literature*

In addition, the supplemental documents listed below generally need to be submitted (template forms are available at http://www.uspto.gov/forms/). The Application Data Sheet (ADS) includes applicant information, claim of priority (e.g., for claiming priority from a provisional patent application, under the "Domestic Benefit" section), assertion of small entity classification (generally allowed for individuals, nonprofit organizations, or businesses ≤500 employees), and any request for no publication of the application (if not filing in foreign countries).

- *Application Data Sheet (ADS – Form SB14 for utility or SB16 for provisional)*
- *Oath and Declaration (Form SB0001)*
- *Information Disclosure Statement (IDS – Form SB08)*

The *abstract* must be only one paragraph (less than 150 words) describing the basic invention in plain language. The *background* section explains the fundamental need that will be addressed by the invention and possibly the most relevant prior art. It is important to not describe any new or novel information about the invention in the background section, since this confuses prior and future novelty. It is also important to limit your description of prior art, since other patent holders could potentially claim that their inventions were misrepresented in your description.

The *summary of the invention* provides a brief overview of the salient points of the invention, and is particularly useful if the *detailed description of the invention* is lengthy. The *description of the invention* should describe the invention or innovation, what it achieves, why it is novel, how it is used, how it is made, and/or a thorough explanation of possible applications. If the description is relatively short, the summary and description are sometimes combined as the same section. Likewise, the brief and detailed sections of *description of the drawings* can be combined if the section is short (and obviously eliminated if there are no drawings). Some patents do not need any drawings; for example, some may instead require chemical or mathematical formulae, or a listing of relevant biologic sequences, or no accessory information at all. The language should be clear to the patent examiner, who is likely familiar with the subject area but not necessarily an expert in the field, and therefore some patents may include a glossary of technical terms, but be careful to not cause problems or limit yourself with overly extensive or detailed definitions.

In the *description of preferred embodiments*, examples may be given to describe specific applications and uses of the invention, starting with the most important feature or version first, and descending down through iterations and alternatives. These examples, referred to as "embodiments," are not always an absolute requirement, but they give clarity and strength to the breadth and specificity of the invention, and will generally be covered in the dependent claims of the application. The patent must be specific enough to allow an expert in the field to replicate and utilize the invention, otherwise the patent examiner may reject the application for "lack of enablement." Also, in an attempt to prevent patents on "theoretical ideas," the patent office has given guidance that patent claims should be specific, credible, and substantial, or in other words, that the invention needs to be "reduced to practice." This means that ideas that are not yet completely studied or developed may not be allowed. However, supporting data can be submitted later during patent prosecution (under rule 132), and therefore you can technically make claims on an invention that may not have yet been built, tested, or proven, but for which you expect to do so. For therapeutic devices and agents, a detailed description of how to construct and use the invention, along with an explanation of the principle mechanism of functionality, is likely sufficient without completing clinical studies, but again, some amount of preliminary evidence or support will likely be needed before the patent is issued.

The claims are the most important part of the application, and as you review patents in your field you will note a very specific legal style of writing used in the claims. Independent claims lay out broad features of the invention, and dependent claims can narrow the specific features or uses of the independent claims. The idea is to write the claims as broad as possible, but also narrow enough that they are allowed by the patent office in light of prior art, novelty, and non-obviousness. Thus claims must take into consideration not only the novelty of the invention itself, but also ways to work around other related patent claims, as well as ways to prevent others from working around your own claims.

The costs of a patent are primarily dependent on the number of independent and dependent claims. For an individual or small business, a patent costs $530 to file (see Table 9), plus an extra cost if there are more than 20 claims ($30 for each claim over 20) or if there are more than three independent claims ($125 for each independent claim over three). Each claim, whether independent or dependent, can only be one sentence and each must be on a separate line. Claims can usually be amended after submission of the patent application as long as they fall within the original specifications laid out in the description of the invention. This is good for those who do not have funding to use a patent attorney, since the patent office will communicate with the patent filer regarding any portions that need revision or reformatting, any documents that may be missing, or any rejections to claims with the opportunity to respond and convince the examiner why claims should be allowed (with or without modification).

Clearly, a patent attorney can be an important asset in successfully obtaining patent protection. An attorney can be hired for the application as a whole, or for specific portions such as the background search or for writing and editing the claims. It is important that the patent attorney have some expertise in the field of the patent. The first draft of a patent application is usually best written by the inventor because he or she will have the most expertise in the invention and can provide the best explanation of what the technology is and why it is important. The attorney can then guide the inventor to edit certain portions or to broaden or narrow certain claims or subject matter in a manner that is most likely to be allowed by the patent office and still provide strong protection.

The background search of prior art is also a very important component because it establishes what has already been done in the relevant field, shows the applicant's expertise in the field, and may sometimes even show that an idea has already been covered or published, thus saving time, cost, and effort for the inventor. Perhaps more importantly, the patent search may also provide ideas and guidance for the best approach to patentability of an idea in a field crowded with similar art. Conducting a patent search can also clarify whether there is "freedom to practice," i.e., whether other prior broad-based patents may affect the ability to use a particular invention even if a patent is granted (more on this below).

Patent examiners expect a reasonable amount of background search to have been performed before filing a patent application. At minimum, a patent search should be conducted in the country where filing, while the most comprehensive searches generally include a detailed review of domestic and foreign patents and patent applications (which may include U.S., Europe, Japan, Canada, Brazil, Russia, India, China, and PCT publications), as well as a literature search in the field of expertise. All relevant material should be cited on the Information Disclosure Statement (IDS), categorized as U.S. patent literature, U.S. patent application literature, foreign patent literature, and non-patent literature.

Patent Drawings

Patent drawings have a specific set of rules, and there are many patent drawing drafters who can complete this work, or you can accomplish it yourself. The fastest way to learn is to simply look at the drawings in the related patents discovered in the background search. In general, figures must be line drawings, black and white only, and must clearly demonstrate the essential views, sections, and/or components of the invention. Different types of hatching may be used to show different depths, materials, sides, or sections. For example, thin parallel lines can be used to represent any variety of depth, perspective, or surface curvature. Drawings must be submitted on standard letter or A4 size paper as a document separate from the text of the patent (or as a separate PDF file through the electronic EFS-web system), with 1-inch page margins and page numbering starting at 1.

Any number of views may be shown to demonstrate embodiments of the invention. Exploded views, partial views, sectional views, or alternate views all have their own rules and specifications. Every possible component of the invention should be labeled with reference numerals, which may use lead lines and arrows. The drawings can be done with the Adobe Illustrator software mentioned above, or with a CAD program such as the popular AutoCAD Inventor, SolidWorks, TurboCAD, or others, but be aware that objects should not be represented as wire-frame views nor as 3D rendered objects (e.g., with scanline, ray tracing, or radiosity rendering).

Some inventions, such as methods, coatings, or chemical compositions, do not require drawings, but it may be beneficial to include drawings anyway if possible. Many other rules and conventions may also apply, as can be found in the Manual of Patent Examining Procedure (MPEP) *Standards for Drawings* or in the NOLO series *How to Make Patent Drawings* by Lo and Pressman.

Assignment & Licensing

A patent owner may choose to practice, sell, assign, or license a patent. An assignment transfers all rights in the patent without limitation, whereas license transfers only certain rights or restrictions on use. Licensing can either be non-exclusive or exclusive, meaning that the patent holder may or may not offer licensing rights to other entities, respectively. In addition, the scope of the license can be broad or narrow, e.g., a broad license to manufacture and distribute a product, or a narrow license for non-commercial use only. In cases where an industry may wish to use a patent as a basis for other technologies, a patent-holder can choose to create an open license, where a standard licensing payment allows anyone to use the technology, thus avoiding the need to negotiate multiple individual agreements.

It is important to note that each inventor listed on the patent owns full rights in the patent and can license or utilize all rights without agreement of other owners, and therefore most companies position themselves as the sole assignee when inventors assign all rights to the company. Many organizations have agreements or contracts with employees that require disclosure of all inventions that pertain to the work and investments of the organization, as well as contracts that assign rights of all inventions to the organization and that have non-compete provisions.

Freedom to operate is an important principle in patent law, and it holds implications for licensing and assignment of patent rights. Patents are considered "exclusionary," meaning that the patent allows the holder to exclude others from utilizing the idea or invention. However, another inventor may still obtain a patent on further improvements to the original invention, but may not have "freedom to practice" the invention without license from the original patent holder.

As a very generic example, imagine an umbrella maker who has a patent on umbrellas, and you obtain a patent for a new type of umbrella handle that can open an umbrella with a button. Without an agreement, you cannot now make umbrellas, nor can the umbrella patent holder use your specific handle. With the assignment or license of rights, however, either through lump sum or continuing royalty payments, you may allow the umbrella maker to use the new handle, or the umbrella maker may allow you to make umbrellas. Thus freedom to operate may be just as important as holding patent rights.

Licensing agreements can have a variety of terms. These may include payment terms (lump sum or royalty payments, and whether the royalty payments are based on a percentage of sales, or are constrained by maximum or minimum amounts, or are simply set payments). The agreement should clearly state whether ownership of intellectual property or company equity is part of the agreement. In addition, the agreement should specify whether the licensor or licensee have rights to subcontract any part of the property or labor to other parties.

Intellectual Property Under Federally-Funded Grants

As discussed previously under the SBIR/STTR grants section, the government may have certain requirements pertaining to inventions that were conceived or developed under federal funding. This may include required disclosure of the invention to the funding agency as well as automatic granting of license or march-in rights for the government to practice the invention should it so choose. Any patent applications that result from federally-funded work must also state that they were supported with federal funds.

Nevertheless, businesses typically retain all intellectual property rights to the technologies they develop under SBIR/STTR, including ownership of all patents, as part of the Bayh-Dole Act. However, the government requires a non-transferable license to practice the invention should it elect to do so, and the inventor must comply with disclosure of all inventions made under SBIR/STTR funding even if the technology began the patent process before the grant was obtained. Failure to report applicable inventions, failure to file patents, or failure to commercialize the technology could theoretically forfeit such rights.

Intellectual property that is conceived, developed, or researched under federal grants needs to be reported through the inter-agency reporting system *iEdison*, found online at https://s-edison.info.nih.gov/iEdison/. This does not apply to research outside the specific stated purposes and activities of the grant. When reporting intellectual property to the government under these grants, you must claim in writing that you elect to retain right and title to the inventions.

To date there are no known instances of SBIR/STTR grants causing loss of IP protection to a company, but the government claims that they may have rights to the technology if it becomes necessary under certain circumstances (such as if the technology provides great public benefit and the business fails to provide it). In fact, the government may control assignments of rights to third parties and could theoretically authorize utilization of patent-protected property in certain circumstances. Therefore this can sometimes create certain concerns for investors and businesses. However, this power is not much different than the general power of the government to utilize any patented technology it deems necessary for the public good (e.g., in times of war, etc.).

On a slightly different note, if a federally-funded project uses sub-contractors, the government does not typically allow the primary awardee company to take ownership of intellectual property created by the sub-contractor as a condition of awarding the sub-contract. This can be a significant issue, but the awardee company and the sub-contractor are allowed to negotiate an agreement of ownership of intellectual property, just technically not as a condition of awarding the sub-contract.

Finally, university professors who develop new inventions are legally considered the inventors, not the university; as the Supreme Court has stated, "rights to an invention belong to the inventor." Therefore most institutions now use strong and detailed language in employment contracts, non-disclosure agreements, and patent assignment, such as the phrase, "I *hereby assign* all rights, title, and interest in all inventions, techniques, discoveries, developments, data, and works of authorship to...." This is due in part to the 2011 Stanford vs. Roche case, where the Supreme Court upheld two important rights of inventors. The first point is that the inventor retains rights to assign ownership of the patent, even in federally-funded inventions. This clarified that the Bayh-Dole Act does not deprive inventors of their rights in an invention. The second point is that when assignment occurs, the language of the agreement is significant: a Stanford professor had signed a contract to "agree to assign" patent rights to the university, but had also signed a non-disclosure agreement with Roche stating "I hereby assign" patent rights. The agreement to "hereby assign" rights trumped the agreement to "assign rights" (presumably at some future point), and therefore Roche won the case. Clearly, it is important to be detailed in what exactly is being assigned and to clarify exact terms and conditions of the agreement.

Non-Disclosure Agreements

Non-disclosure agreements (NDAs) are used for a wide variety of purposes, and many free templates can be found online for a variety of situations. As mentioned above, NDAs are used to prevent public disclosure of confidential information, and can also assign title and rights to inventions made by collaboration and agreement. It is important for NDAs to clearly define the confidential information and what it may be used for. Remember to request renewal of agreements if necessary, and to request return or destruction of confidential information at the end of the agreement. You may also want to consider non-compete, sublicensing, exclusive licensing, or conflict of interest agreements. NDAs typically have the provisions listed in Table 11.

Table 11: Outline of a non-disclosure agreement.

Parties:

Individuals/companies entering into the legal agreement

Disclosure:

Definition of confidential information.

Purpose of the disclosure.

Agreement of parties to disclose/receive confidential information.

Confidentiality:

Agreement to not use confidential information except for specific purposes stated in the agreement.

Agreement to not disclose confidential information.

Agreement to protect the secrecy of confidential information.

Limits on Confidential Information:

No obligation or fault if information became public through no wrongful act, through no breech of agreement, through a third party, or through legal order.

Ownership of Confidential Information:

Details of any assignment or transfer of right, title, or license, or disclaimer of any implied transfer.

Term and Termination:

Term of binding agreement, rights, and obligations.

Rights to seek injunction and equitable relief.

Rights for return or destruction of confidential information

§

PART IV – REGULATORY ISSUES

"It is in fact nothing short of a miracle that
modern methods of instruction have not yet
entirely strangled the holy curiosity of inquiry."
Albert Einstein, autobiographical notes,
Albert Einstein: Philosopher-Scientist

"Only someone who is not seeking is safe from error."
Albert Einstein, *Letter to Gustav Bucky 1945*

"Every artist was first an amateur."
Ralph Waldo Emerson
Letters and Social Aims: Progress of Culture

General Business

Almost every company, especially in technology, has some level of regulatory oversight. The following is a brief overview of some ways to prepare for regulatory issues that may arise, with descriptions of policies and paperwork that may pertain to certain companies, but be aware that every industry and field will have its own specific rules and regulations that may not be covered in detail here. Special attention is given to government funding regulations and the FDA regulatory processes for drugs, devices, and biologic agents. The last section relates to healthcare reimbursement rules and strategies.

The lists of these regulations can seem overwhelming, but for the most part, anyone who keeps good documentation and is careful to conduct safe research and make quality products will find that he or she is already in compliance. In many cases, compliance is simply a matter of keeping good records and having company documentation of protocols for quality assurance and quality control. The discussion below is intended as a guide so that as your company grows you can check this list to see if any standards may be applicable or need implementing.

As a general employer, the company is mandated by federal law to visibly display the poster "Equal Employment Opportunity Is The Law." Additional notices to employees may also be required, depending on the nature of your business and the number of employees in the business, such as "Fair Labor Standards Act," "Contract Work Hours and Safety Standards Act," "Service Contract Act and Public Contracts Act," and "Family and Medical Leave Act." The state may require additional postings to workers, including "Equal Employment Opportunity," "Occupational Safety and Health – Job Safety and Health Protection," "Unemployment Insurance – Notice to Workers," and "Worker's Compensation Insurance Notice."

Engineering & Defense

For engineering and defense work, many different standards may be applicable (see Table 12), but exact certifications and standards will likely depend on who the customers is and what that customer or regulatory agency requires. ISO9000/ISO9001 certification is becoming a common standard, although many companies choose to remain ISO-compliant rather than formally ISO-certified due to administrative burdens. Many other possible ISO standards may apply to engineering and manufacturing depending on the particular industry and application—an overview of ISO standards can be found at http://www.iso.org/iso/iso_catalogue/catalogue_ics.htm. In addition to ISO standards, electronics technology is covered by IEC standards and telecommunication technology is covered by ITU standards.

If manufacturing products for the Department of Defense (DOD), the products may need to comply with military standards (MIL-STD). Again, the particular buyer or contractor will typically notify you if products need to comply with these standards, but it may be good to be aware of them while designing, testing, and building new technologies. These standards specify details about products for military use, including design, manufacture, testing, and performance standards. This is to validate that product design accurately performs the specified function, that the product maintains reliability under a variety of conditions over time, and that products are consistent amongst batches. This may therefore require material controls, design controls, manufacturing controls, documentation and reporting controls, and corrective and preventative action protocols. Environmental stress testing is often performed on engineered devices to ensure quality performance over time, including accelerated life testing (HALT/HASS compliance). Further details can be found in the MIL-HDBK, MIL-STD, MIL-SPEC, MIL-PRF, and MIL-DTL documents.

Table 12: Potential regulations pertaining to DOD and engineering work.
- International Traffic in Arms (ITAR) regulations and State Department registration and compliance for DOD products
- Certified Information Systems Security Professional (CISSP)
- ISO, IEC, and/or ITU standards
- Information Assurance Workforce Improvement Program (DOD 8570) certification and accreditation
- Military Standards (MIL-STD) for testing and engineering
- Possible air sterility, particle regulations, and water purification requirements
- FD&C Act section 513-514 for product controls and performance standards
- Radiation Control for Health and Safety Act (RCHSA)

Health Research

Table 13 shows regulations that might apply to any health research business. These regulations will likely not be absolute unless you receive certain federal funding or contracts with the government, or if your product will require FDA approval (in which case the regulations that may apply are discussed in more detail in their respective sections).

Table 13: Potential regulations pertaining to health products, healthcare, diagnostics, biotechnology, pharmaceutical agents, and medical devices (in addition to those discussed in their respective sections).
- Compliance with Code of Federal Regulations (CFR) [Discussed in detail in the *SBIR/STTR Grants* section and the *FDA Regulatory Approval Processes* sections]:

- Drugs – 21 CFR 200-300
- Biologics – 21 CFR 600
- Devices – 21 CFR 800-1000
- Tissues – 21 CFR 1271
- National Provider Identifier (NPI) registration [both institutional and personal for healthcare providers]
- Human research training [e.g., the NIH provides some modules and a company can provide its own training, see http://www.hhs.gov/ohrp/education/training/introduction.html and http://www.cc.nih.gov/training/training.html]
  - Certificate of Protecting Human Subject Research Participants (PHRP)
  - Certificate of Clinical Research
  - Inclusion of Children Policy [for any human research]
  - Human Subjects Assurance [for any human subjects research, available on NIH modules, see http://grants.nih.gov/grants/policy/hs/index.htm and http://www.hhs.gov/ohrp]
- Animal research training modules [via Office of Laboratory Animal Welfare (OLAW)]
  - Vertebrate and/or Nonvertebrate Animal Welfare Assurances
  - Animal welfare training [see http://grants.nih.gov/grants/olaw/tutorial/index.htm]
  - Institutional Animal Care and Use Committees (IACUC) approval
  - Use of Laboratory Animals statement
  - See http://grants.nih.gov/grants/olaw/sampledoc/index.htm for assurance template
  - See http://grants.nih.gov/grants/olaw/olaw.htm for more information
- International Conference on Harmonization [some training modules are provided by the NIH or other institutions]
  - Good Laboratory Practice (GLP)
  - Good Clinical Practice (GCP)
  - Good Manufacturing Practice (GMP)
- FD&C Act section 513-514 for product controls and performance standards

- Radiation Control for Health and Safety Act (RCHSA)
- Hazard Analysis and Critical Control Points (HACCP) for food safety analysis and food processing.

Table 14 is a general list of business documentation that will likely be required if conducting clinical research or if work is federally funded (such as with SBIR/STTR grants). Of course, these policies can be adopted by any company. All documents (such as company policies, rules, regulations, compliances, assurances, and certifications) should be assembled into a company manual for reference and auditing purposes.

Table 14: General business documentation for federally-funded research or clinical studies.
- Assurance of Compliance with Civil Rights, Rehabilitation, and Discrimination Acts [e.g., file the HHS690 form with the Office for Civil Rights of the federal agency funding a project]
- Financial Conflict of Interest Policy [The NIH provides federal guidelines on conflict of interest in research, and instructions and tutorial are available at http://grants.nih.gov/grants/policy/coi/, and many templates are available online.]
- Statement of Impact of Grant Activities on the Environment and Historic Properties
- Institutional Debarment and Suspension Assurance
- Lobbying Assurance
- Non-Delinquency on Federal Debt Assurance
- PI Assurance (individual grant application assurances)
- Prohibited Research Certification
- Recombinant DNA and Human Gene Transfer Research Certification
- Research Misconduct Policy [Many templates available online, or see file reflecting U.S. Department of Health and Human Services Public Health Service Policies on Research Misconduct – Final Rule, Code of Federal Regulations, Vol. 42, Part 93]
- Office of Research Integrity Statement [submit to ORI, template found at http://ori.hhs.gov/small-organization-statement]
- Research Using Human Embryonic Stem Cells Certification
- Research on Transplantation of Human Fetal Tissue Certificatioin
- Select Agent Research Certification
- Smoke Free Workplace Certification

- Drug Free Workplace Assurance
- Copy of Federal Acquisition Regulations (FAR 31.2) for reference and auditing
- Federal Wide Assurance (FWA) with Office for Human Research Protections (OHRP)
- IRB Approvals
- Independent Data Safety Monitoring Board (DSMB)
- Public Health Service Policies and Procedures on Research Misconduct
- Statement for Small Organizations on Dealing with Allegations of Research Misconduct
- Financial Disclosure of Clinical Investigators (21 CFR 54)
- Also see the "Human Research" and "Animal Research" parts in the preceding Table 13.

For conducting clinical trials, every clinical study protocol will need IRB approval. Private entities can use contracted IRB's like the Western IRB or Chesapeake IRB, amongst others. Protocols generally require some form of certification and/or training of an organization's investigators in some combination of clinical research, ethics, protection of human subjects, informed consent, human subjects assurance, vulnerable patient populations, and HIPAA (the NIH provides training or certification modules on many of these topics). IRB templates are specific to each IRB; the general information found in an IRB is covered in this OHSR outline: http://ohsr.od.nih.gov/info/sheet5.html.

FDA human trials require a reference to the study on www.clinicaltrials.gov, including interventions that involve drugs, biologics, or devices, or studies under an IND or IDE. This does not include, however, feasibility studies, uncontrolled studies, or prototype studies of devices, or phase I studies of drugs.

Clinical study forms include "Informed Consent" or "Consent to Participate in Research Study," which should include elements in 21 CFR 50.25 and 45 CFR 46.116. This includes describing the purpose of the study, the risks and benefits, why the patient is being asked to be in the study, length of the study, voluntary participation, how any treatments deviate from standard care, any randomization in the study (including chances of receiving experimental treatment or placebo), expected involvement and commitments involved with completing the study, follow-up care, release of results of the study, protocols for adverse outcomes, reimbursements for participation, who will have access to patient information, ability to withdraw from the study, and contact information if there are questions or concerns.

The IRB review boards will want to see detailed descriptions of every aspect involved with the study, as well as all documentation that will be provided to the patients. A broad overview of a clinical trial protocol template can be found in Appendix IV: this is based on FDA requirements for drugs, biologics, and/or devices. Other templates may be provided by individual universities or clinical research organizations. In addition, various guidance documents and templates can be found under specific agencies, either at specific institutes of the NIH, at the FDA website: http://www.fda.gov/, or in ICH E1-E12 documentation on ICH.org. Note that for applicable FDA regulatory trials, the following statement must now be included in the Informed Consent:

> "A description of this clinical trial will be available on www.clinicaltrials.gov, as required by U.S. Law. This website will not include information that can identify you. At most, the website will include a summary of the results. You can search this website at any time."

When seeking to enter clinical use, both devices and drugs are subject to *Good Laboratory Practice* (GLP), *Good Manufacturing Practice* (GMP), and/or *Good Clinical Practice* (GCP). GCP is defined by the International Conference on Harmonization (ICH), which seeks to enhance the safety, quality, efficacy, and ethicality of human research endeavors. GCP is explained in the FDA's 45 CFR part 46 and 21 CFR parts 11, 50, 54, 56 for general rules (and also see the ICH E6 documentation on the ICH.org website)... as well as parts 312, 314, 320 for drugs... and parts 812, 814 for devices (also see ISO 14155 standards regarding clinical investigation of devices).

Likewise, GLP basically ensures that all studies are clearly documented and that facilities are safe and adequate for the studies being done; further details are defined in the FDA's 21 CFR part 58. Lastly, GMP ensures safety and consistency in the manufacturing process (and is also referred to in *Quality System* regulation (QS)), but note that many types of medical devices may be exempt. GMP is defined in 21 CFR part 210 for drugs and 820 for devices (also see ISO 13485 standards for quality systems management of devices).

The choice of clinical data management software is important for a high-quality clinical study, and there are many options available. The software should be capable of organizing (and preferably analyzing) the data parameters required for the study, and should be able to utilize data formats from all the various clinical study centers and any other associated data systems. One popular system used in academic, industry, and government is the SAS data management system, which can process data used in pharmaceutical, biotech, and device studies. For less complex studies, such as those used for some device studies, other database management systems may be adequate (e.g., Microsoft Access), but data should generally be password protected, encrypted, and auditable for any changes in data. Other helpful functions may include indexing, data entry integrity, data compression, data mining, programming interfaces, and online analytical processing and reporting (SAS holding a potential advantage in this regard over other systems like Oracle). See 21 CFR part 11 for FDA guidance on clinical database systems.

FDA REGULATORY APPROVAL PROCESSES

Devices, drugs, and biologic compounds for human benefit are regulated by the FDA. Regulatory rules and processes are defined by the first chapter of Title 21 of the Code of Federal Regulations, which can be found online in their full form, but are summed up here much more concisely. Specifically, pharmaceuticals are described in the 21 CFR 200-300 series, biologics are described in the 600 series, and devices are described in the 800-1000 series (with cell- and tissue-based products described in section 1271).

The FDA classifies new products as drug, device, or biologic, and assigns them to the respective center, namely, the Center for Drug Evaluation and Research (CDER), the Center for Devices and Radiologic Health (CDRH), or the Center for Biologics Evaluation and Research (CBER). A product may fall into a combination of these categories, as discussed below under *Combination Products*.

Rather than acquiring internal staffing and resources for clinical studies, many companies use contract research organizations (CROs) to carry out studies for both device and drug approval processes. The CRO works with study sites on study management, IRB processes, patient recruitment, data collection, study reporting, study site auditing, and core laboratory usage. CROs vary in the extent and depth of services offered, so it is important to find an organization that has knowledge and experience with your specific field, such as particular pharmaceutical or medical device experience. Despite the fact that there are over a thousand CROs, the majority of clinical studies are done only through a few of the largest. Likewise, for manufacturing these products, the choice of a reliable contract manufacturing organization (CMO) can be important to a company's quality and success. Even some large pharmaceutical and device companies have moved to conducting pre-clinical research, clinical investigations, and manufacturing operations through CROs and CMOs. The FDA considers all responsibility for research and manufacturing integrity to remain with the sponsoring company.

<u>Devices</u>

Medical devices fall into one of three classifications, listed below. These classifications are based on intended use, indicated use, and risks of use.

Class I devices are those that present minimal risk and cannot be intended for significant support of life or prevention of significant illness or injury (e.g., wound bandages). These may qualify for exemption as described below.

Class II devices are those that are more significant in support of health or prevention of disease or injury, and may have elevated risks of an adverse event (e.g., IV infusion pumps). These may also qualify for exemption as described below.

Class III devices generally are those that support important life functions, prevent significant illness, or have significant risk of adverse events (e.g., cardiac pacemakers). This includes any device that is "not substantially equivalent" to existing medical devices.

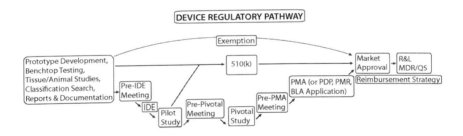

Class I and II devices can use the Premarket Notification (PMN) pathway, also known as the 510(k) pathway, for FDA approval. The 510(k) process requires "substantial equivalence" of the device to another FDA-approved device in terms of use, efficacy, and safety. Class III devices, on the other hand, must use the Premarket Approval (PMA) pathway. It is not always definite what classification will be assigned by the FDA, and therefore communicating with the administrators of the CDRH throughout the process is important. The FDA provides a method of classifying your device (including whether the device may receive exemption, or whether it is considered a medical device at all) at: http://www.fda.gov/MedicalDevices/DeviceRegulationandGuidance/Overvie w/ClassifyYourDevice/default.htm

An Investigational Device Exemption (IDE) is used to gather clinical data on the device prior to submitting a PMA or 510(k) application. Clinical data will be required for all PMA applications, but for relatively few 510(k) applications (see the two converging branches of the 510(k) pathway above—the "pilot study" may also be a feasibility, proof-of-concept, or comparative study). An IDE application requires much less detail than the 510(k) or PMA application. All devices that do not meet exemption criteria will require some amount of testing, whether bench-top analysis, animal testing, or modeled preclinical testing. The CDRH provides guidance on what types of data are required for a 510(k) application. A "de novo process" for 510(k) applications may allow certain devices that do not have a predicate device but that likely have safety comparable to class I or II devices to proceed under the 510(k) pathway rather than the PMA, and this will certainly necessitate the IDE route through 510(k).

When submitting a device for consideration, you can request an early collaboration meeting with the CDRH to clarify plans and requirements for a specific product. If clinical data will be required, or if new to the process, it is typical to request a pre-IDE meeting. As much material and information should be prepared as possible, including the application, proposal, study design, device manuals, and supporting data, as well as any plans for studies outside the U.S. The IDE study design should involve a clinical study that will be IRB-approved, with informed consent, monitoring, and result reporting, and should include device labeling that states, "For Investigational Use Only."

Different devices will obviously have different requirements; it is worth reviewing the generic IDE template in Appendix V and the Clinical Protocol Template in Appendix IV for guidance on what aspects may need to be included in an application for IDE. The reviewers provide feedback on whether the study design is adequate or whether any additional laboratory or animal data is needed before starting the IDE. The recommendations made at this meeting are not binding, but if you do not follow them the same objections will likely later be raised in study reviews, costing significant time and money. The IDE application can then be submitted for formal review, and it should then only take 30 days to obtain approval for beginning investigational studies. More information on IDE requirements can be found in 21 CFR 812.

Under the IDE, a pilot study is conducted, followed by a larger pivotal study phase for class III devices. The pilot study generally involves a few dozen subjects at one or more centers, and based on these results, the CDRH may make updated recommendations on study design, endpoint definitions, patient populations, control groups, and/or other data variables that should be acquired. For unprecedented high-risk devices, this will likely involve the use of the gold standard of prospective randomized controlled trials, comparing the device either to standard of care practice, best medical treatment, or placebo. But devices that have related precedent devices, even including some class III devices, may qualify simply for a series of clinical case reports. The case series may be compared to historical treatment outcomes using previously published data on safety and efficacy of similar treatment or diagnostic devices. The company should choose the least burdensome study design which still provides data that satisfies the FDA (a primary purpose of the pre-IDE meeting). Devices generally only need to show non-inferiority rather than superiority.

When planning for PMA review, you should request a pre-pivotal meeting after obtaining the pilot study data under the IDE. At this meeting you can review all the data with the CDRH, having a detailed and interactive review of the device, discussion of any concerns of major or minor deficiencies, and also confirmation of the appropriate study design for the pivotal studies. You should try to anticipate any concerns or questions that the CDRH will have regarding the device. The extent of clinical study complexity and duration will be determined based on the intended use of the device, its mechanism of operation, and its safety profile. The FDA also provides "Design Considerations for Pivotal Clinical Investigations for Medical Devices" at http://www.fda.gov/downloads/MedicalDevices/DeviceRegulationandGuidan ce/GuidanceDocuments/UCM267831.pdf.

A PMA review for market approval usually takes around 6 months if there are no concerns or objections. The review of the 510(k) application determines whether adequate supporting data exists and whether the device indeed qualifies for "substantial equivalence," and this review takes about 3 months if there are no concerns or objections. There are fees for both 510(k) and PMA processes. Updated listings of fees can be found at: http://www.fda.gov/MedicalDevices/DeviceRegulationandGuidance/HowtoM arketYourDevice/PremarketSubmissions/PremarketApprovalPMA/ucm048161 .htm.

There are several approaches to filing a PMA. With a *traditional PMA*, the entire application is submitted at once. In a *modular PMA*, separate components of the PMA application can be submitted as they are completed, which can be helpful for small companies that have devices in early stages and that benefit from ongoing feedback from the FDA. This should not be used, however, when the device design may be later modified or if the device is nearly ready for PMA submission.

If a class III device has multiple similar devices that are well-studied by the FDA, it may qualify for *streamlined PMA*. Similarly, devices that have been frequently reviewed by the FDA may qualify for the *Product Development Protocol* (PDP), which is like a PMA but also establishes early, clear, and predictable milestones and pre-agreed upon results that must be met for market approval. The company can then provide reports at its own pace as the data is collected, and once the milestones and results have been met the device is considered to have completed the PMA. A *Premarket Report* (PMR) is the same application as a PMA, but is specifically for reprocessable single-use devices (e.g., products that can optionally be disposed of after use or cleaned and reused), and unlike the PMA, the PMR does not need to disclose principles of operation or the methods or controls used in the manufacturing of the device. A *Biologic Licensing Application* (BLA), discussed further below, is essentially the biologic equivalent of filing the PMA.

A general 510(k) application structure is shown in Appendix VI. The PMA contains similar components, as well as additional elements found in the Clinical Protocol Template of Appendix IV. Most important in the PMA is the detailed description of the device, its functions, its intended use, preclinical study data and protocols, clinical study data and protocols, manufacturing methods, labeling, instructions for use, and many other aspects. The FDA does not dictate PMA structure but states that the PMA application must include "study protocols, safety and efficacy data, adverse reactions and complications, device failures and replacements, patient information, patient complaints, tabulations of data from all individual subjects, results of statistical analyses, and any other information from the clinical investigations," as well as "microbiology, toxicology, immunology, biocompatibility, stress, wear, shelf life, and other laboratory or animals tests." All lab studies need to have complied with Good Laboratory Practices (21 CFR part 58).

In addition, the device must also meet good manufacturing practice (GMP) standards. Certain class I devices may be exempt from this GMP standard. Class I and II devices that have not significantly changed since before 1976 may be considered a *pre-amendment device*, meaning that they may receive exemption from the 510(k) process and/or GMP requirements. Certain class I and II devices may receive exemption of the 510(k) process and/or GMP requirements based on their nature and FDA classification (about three fourths of class I devices are exempt from the PMN review process). Device exemptions for PMN and GMP standards are listed at http://www.accessdata.fda.gov/scripts/cdrh/cfdocs/cfpcd/315.cfm. The specific requirements of GMP standards are detailed in 21 CFR part 820. It may also be useful to look into the Division of Small Manufacturers International and Consumer Assistance (DSMICA), which helps small device companies comply with FDA manufacturing standards and also grants fee waivers for small-business PMA applications. Implantable devices will likely need to show a biocompatibility analysis as described in ISO 10993 standards.

The FDA allows a *Humanitarian Device Exemption* (HDE) as an expedited approval process for class III devices whose indications would result in the device being used in less than 4000 patients per year. An HDE still requires proof of safety, IRB approvals, and ongoing monitoring, but clinical study sample size and duration may be much less. Likewise, a *treatment IDE* may be granted for a device, allowing it to be used on patients with life-threatening conditions that have no adequate treatment options, even before the device obtains marketing approval. The treatment IDE allows a device to be used in patients outside controlled clinical studies, even while the device may be simultaneously under investigation in clinical studies, as long as it is for a possible life-threatening situation, but IRB approval is still necessary and patient insurance will likely not cover any costs.

After receiving market approval, the business must register and list the device with the FDA (this is called *R&L* for "registration and listing," see http://www.fda.gov/Training/CDRHLearn/ucm176506.htm for more details and current annual fees). You cannot register the business until you have begun the application process, and generally must register within 30 days of FDA clearance. Subsequent to market approval, the business must conduct medical device reporting (MDR) and continue to comply with quality systems regulation (QS), involving GMP and device monitoring and record keeping.

Manufacturers and distributors are not required to file annual certifications, but complaint files must be maintained, and user facilities must file an annual report to summarize any adverse events. Any device malfunctions or serious injuries or deaths associated with medical devices must be reported to the FDA (using the applicable form 3500A, 3417, 3419, and/or 3381).

Clearly, the business sponsor should seek the most cost-effective and expedited process possible for the device. Some companies choose to first conduct research for a new device outside the U.S. because IRB review boards and FDA initial reviews can add 6-12 months to the time needed for clinical data collection compared to other countries. In addition, some institutions can add to the bureaucracy of contract negotiations and IRB approvals. Study sites will likely each have their own research contract terms, which may include various cost agreements, and may also carry indemnity clauses or assignment of intellectual property clauses that you should beware of. It is helpful to review data from clinical study sites to ensure that study centers are adequately managing and prioritizing your research study. In some cases of class III devices, a pivotal study may require hundreds or possibly even thousands of patients, and obtaining this many patients can require many research sites, each of which needs its own contracts and IRB approvals, requiring significant time and resources.

FDA regulations on medical devices are provided in the 21 CFR 800 series. Notable sections include part 801 (labeling), 803 (reporting), 807 (establishment registration, device listing, & 510(k) PMN), 812 (IDE), 814 (PMA), and 820 (subchapter H). Other standards for device use, sterility, packaging, etc. are ASTM D1585, ASTM F2097, ASTM F2459, ASTM F2847, ASTM E2314, EN 868, as well as ISO 11607, ISO 13485, ISO 14971, ICS 11.100.20, ICS 11.040.01, IEC 60601-1 (electrical devices), and IEC 62304 (software) standards. Useful resources include several guidance documents at http://www.fda.gov/MedicalDevices/DeviceRegulationandGuidance/Guidance Documents/default.htm, and searchable databases of device information at http://www.accessdata.fda.gov/scripts/cdrh/cfdocs/search/search.cfm. Further guidance is given for FDA rules and regulations of medical devices at http://www.fda.gov/MedicalDevices/DeviceRegulationandGuidance/Overvie w/default.htm.

Drugs

The process of drug development has evolved extensively over the last few decades. It is no coincidence that the pharmaceutical industry really began to grow around the same time that the molecular functions of the cell began to be understood in the 1940s and '50s. Targeted drug screening expanded the arsenal of drugs from simple antibiotics and heart medications to a much wider array of medications. The advent of the biotechnology industry then advanced more complex therapeutic approaches beyond just small molecule pharmaceuticals, creating highly targeted biologic agents and interesting new approaches to treating diseases. It is incredible to think that the biotech industry achieved its first commercial success only in the 1980s, when Genentech produced the first approved biotechnology drugs, namely, recombinant human insulin and human growth hormone.

Although biotech and pharma startup companies rarely have all the resources to develop and commercialize their products from the ground up, they can follow the early model of Genentech and many other companies in licensing rights to larger pharmaceutical companies or partnering with more specialized entities, thereby generating revenue and resources in early stages of the startup company while also supplementing the product pipelines of larger companies. Due to increased recognition of inherent risks and attenuated interest from investors, biotech and pharma companies are rarely able to use an IPO as a sole means of raising cash, instead depending more on rounds of venture capital financing, private investment offerings, investment banks, licensing agreements, partnerships, debts, and/or grants.

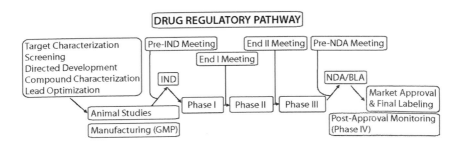

Drug development has been aided recently by better high-throughput assays and genome-based analytical methods. In addition, pharmacogenomics and pharmacoproteomics have enabled better drug targeting. Ideally, the disease process and drug target are identified and characterized prior to screening, and targeted compounds can be developed by directing knowledge of disease mechanisms back towards a therapeutic agent, rather than screening numerous drug candidates through artificial model systems.

For this reason, targeted biologic agents hold tremendous potential as future treatments for many diseases and conditions that have no other therapeutic options, leaving the door wide open for further advancements in biotechnology and healthcare. Bioengineered molecules and cells, along with more advanced molecular delivery systems, will likely provide much more safe and effective therapies in the future.

Due to the complex variables involved in drug safety and efficacy, the FDA has sponsored cooperative research grants in the regulatory science itself. For example, this includes addressing new ideas in clinical trial design, better characterization of nanoparticles, or new strategies to predict safety and efficacy using a small heart and lung model. These focus areas will likely adjust over time. The NCATS seeks to be involved in funding improved models for screening toxicity of compounds and for analyzing prospective risk factors in clinical trial data. For more information on small-business biotechnology resources, see the *Additional Resources* under the *Grants* section.

Once a compound is shown to be a likely therapeutic candidate, the sponsoring company typically requests a pre-IND meeting with the CDER to discuss the plan for the new compound, particularly if the company is new to the process. A letter should be sent to the FDA, generally including chemical information, intended indications, and intended objectives of the meeting, including detailed information of pre-clinical data, clinical study plans, and manufacturing information. The pre-IND meeting is typically scheduled within 2 months of the request, and the meeting itself should occur at least six months before submitting the IND. Further details on FDA meetings for drug development can be found at the following link: http://www.fda.gov/downloads/Drugs/GuidanceComplianceRegulatoryInfor mation/Guidances/ucm153222.pdf.

The *Investigational New Drug* (IND) application is then submitted to the FDA by a sponsoring organization or an individual sponsoring investigator. Because of needed financing and publication of data, patents are filed well before the IND. As with devices, FDA regulatory fees for small businesses may be waived, particularly for those that do not yet have a product on the market or those where financing is a barrier to advancing a potentially beneficial product.

The FDA will review the IND application and decide whether clinical investigation may proceed or whether there are concerns that require further pre-clinical investigation. The FDA assembles a Pharmaceutical Data Sheet (PDS) for investigational agents. As with devices, Good Manufacturing Process (GMP) must be used in making the test drug. Preclinical data is used to create a starting dose and dosing schedule, usually based on a variety of formulas that depend on animal pharmacokinetics, "maximal tolerated dose," "no adverse effects" dose, and/or dosing of similar agents that are already on the market. Dosing schedules may range from single bolus to continuous infusion.

Approval of the IND allows human subject research to commence. A drug must pass through three phases of studies before receiving market approval, and each phase may require a couple years to complete. A Phase I study is usually conducted at one or more institutions, and is exclusively for determining safety and any adverse effects. This data is used to form dosing parameters for any Phase II trial. As such, Phase I studies may have multiple primary and secondary objectives (safe dose, effective dose, toxic dose, side effects, signs of toxicity, signs of therapeutic activity, etc.).

For dosage parameters, several methods of dose escalation may be used, including intra-patient dose escalation or graded dosages amongst different patient groups, each done until adverse effects are observed. Phase I participants must typically have a disease that is not effectively treated with any standard treatment options. Sub-analysis may be done based on gender, ethnicity, pre-existing organ failure, or other subgroups. Phase I data is also used to determine pharmacokinetics (absorption, distribution, metabolism, excretion), optimal dosing schedules, and routes of administration. Meetings with the FDA can provide guidance on trial design and methodology prior to and during the clinical trial phases. After completion of Phase I, an "End-of-

Phase-I" meeting is held with the FDA to determine whether the study may continue to Phase II, including any concerns or suggestions with proceeding.

A "Phase IB" trial may be used to study a combination of drug therapies. The original drug is first tested in Phase I, then combined with other targeted agents in Phase IB. The combination may sometimes be approved in an IND for a Phase I alone if the new agent does not have bioactivity of its own but enhances that of another agent (such as in chemotherapy drugs).

The design of the phase II study further addresses the dosing and schedules, the measures that will be used to gauge therapeutic effects, the specific diseases that will be admissible, the timeline for expected therapeutic effects, the number of patients to enroll to detect significance, the methods and schedule of interim data analysis, the exclusion/inclusion criteria for subjects, and even the scale-up manufacturing of the agent. The study protocol should clearly identify its objectives and the hypotheses that it intends to test. The protocol must justify its design and statistical methods. The maximum number of patients should be stated and justified based on expected type I and type II statistical errors. There should also be a specific stopping point for the trial in the case of any negative outcomes (see Appendix IV for more details of a clinical study). A phase II study may be divided, with the first portion finalizing dosage, schedules, data parameters, and endpoints, and where the second portion focuses more on safety and efficacy data in preparation for Phase III. As with device pilot and pivotal studies, a phase II study may have hundreds of patients and a phase III may have well over a thousand patients.

Randomized controlled studies are the gold standard for drug studies. These are typically conducted by contract research organizations (CROs) at multi-center sites or cooperative groups. IRB approval must typically be given at each study site or institution. The study should also provide for internal controls, quality assurance, and frequent scientific and statistical review. The sites and institutions may use internal or affiliate health-care providers. The FDA requires reporting of all adverse events, protocol amendments, protocol status changes, protocol deviations, and any periodic study results or publications. The FDA is also requiring laboratory assays or clinical imaging if it is applicable to the agent or disease being tested. Subjects in Phase II are generally functional, without organ dysfunction, and not at an end-point of disease.

Phase III should be preceded by a detailed review with the FDA of all previous data on the drug and further defined study protocols (this is the "End-of-Phase-II" meeting). Depending on the intended applications of the new drug, the FDA may require that Phase II and/or Phase III studies not compare the test treatment to just placebo but to a currently-used standard-of-care therapy. The therapeutic agent must typically show statistically-significant and clinically-significant superior effect over controls in at least two Phase III clinical trials, unless a single well-performed study shows particularly striking results. The use of a Data and Safety Monitoring Board is now required in these trials.

The therapeutic agent must show both efficacy and safety, weighing the risks of side effects versus benefits of therapy. When this is demonstrated, the sponsor should have a "pre-NDA meeting" to discuss any questions or concerns and ensure completeness of the submission data. Thereafter the sponsor should submit a New Drug Application (NDA) or Biologic License Application (BLA). The time for the FDA to review this application can vary significantly, but the time for review is added back to market exclusivity provisions provided by the Hatch-Waxman Act.

Market approval of a product allows the company to market their product to the public, and also endows physicians with the power to prescribe the product not just for the indicated treatment, but for any purpose they choose, though physicians may be somewhat limited by their scope of practice, the currently accepted standard of care, and the threat of lawsuits. Importantly, the company must continue to conduct and report follow-up studies on the drug after market approval (often called Phase IV monitoring).

For therapeutic agents that would be unprofitable to produce or that would treat a disease affecting fewer than 200,000 people in the U.S. (which could include about 6,000 different diseases), the Orphan Drug Act offers assistance, including tax breaks (~50% of costs), research grants (through the Office of Orphan Products Development - OOPD), and a seven year marketing monopoly (for both patentable and unpatentable therapies) to the company as an incentive to develop such drugs. Research guidance may also be provided by the Center for Drug Evaluation and Research (CDER) and Center for Biologic Evaluation and Research (CBER). Applications for Orphan Drug

Designation must be filed before filing a New Drug Application (NDA) or Product License Application (PLA).

A similar but separate pathway is *accelerated approval* (subpart E), which allows therapies for severe, life-threatening conditions to be used clinically before safety and efficacy have been established, with the requirement that safety, efficacy, and endpoint objectives continue to be closely monitored and reported. This is different than *fast-track approval*, which uses the standard drug approval system but may allow agreement with the FDA about use of surrogate markers in the study rather than definitive endpoints, and may also allow the NDA or BLA to be submitted in separate components over time, similar to the modular PMA for devices. This is also different from a *treatment IND* (previously called *compassionate use*), which allows an investigational agent to be used for treatment of life-threatening conditions with no adequate therapeutic options on patients not enrolled in clinical trials. This may be done either concurrently with or outside of phase I-III controlled studies, although an IRB review is still necessary and costs are not covered by insurance.

The Hatch-Waxman Act provides up to five-year exclusivity for newly approved new molecular entities (NMEs). An *Abbreviated NDA* is filed when creating a generic version of an existing drug, and this act ensures that the original drug must be off-patent (or claimed invalid) before the generic may enter the market. If the original patent is declared invalid, there is still a 30-month waiting period before a generic can enter the market. Interestingly, the act allows that an original drug can receive an extension term of patent protection equal to half the time spanning from the start of human clinical trials of the IND to the submission of the NDA, plus the entire time of NDA review (up to five years combined maximum). This act also allows 14 years of market exclusivity once the drug is approved. See the *Utility Patent* section for more information on drug utility patents.

The Hatch-Waxman Act also provides incentives to generic drug companies by limiting the FDA to only be able to request bioavailability studies on a generic drug application (which studies can be conducted under the Hatch-Waxman Act even while the original drug is still under patent protection, based on the experimental-use privilege discussed under the *Utility Patent* section). The Act also governs the bioequivalence between brand and generic drugs to allow up to 20% variability in bioavailability, and also permits the first maker of a generic drug to have six months of market exclusivity with the generic form. Many revisions in the act have been proposed and will likely amend the act over the coming years. As mentioned in the *Utility Patent* section, drugs may also be protected by conducting new trials of the drug in pediatric patients (allowing up to 1 year exclusivity) or for obtaining over-the-counter (OTC) status (allowing up to 3 years of additional exclusivity). Alternatively, drugs can gain an edge over competitors after patent by simply applying for new drug indications ("repurposing") or by reformulating the drug.

Additional guidance documents are provided by the FDA at http://www.fda.gov/Drugs/DevelopmentApprovalProcess/default.htm and http://www.fda.gov/Drugs/GuidanceComplianceRegulatoryInformation/Guidances/default.htm. Other important legislative and regulatory provisions, such as general business law, patent law, grant funding rules, securities regulations, etc., are discussed in their respective sections.

Combination Products

With the advent of many novel innovations, there will most certainly be more inventions that are classified by the FDA as *combination products*. One example is the drug-eluting stent which is both a device and a drug. (Note that the term "combination product" is also sometimes used to refer to dual drug compounds, but here refers to a product that falls into two or more regulated components of drug, device, or biologic agent.) Unfortunately there is not always a definite path for these unique products, and each aspect of the product must still be approved through the applicable agency.

Congress mandated the creation of the Office of Combination Products (OCP) in the FDA in 2002. Through the OCP, a company may request, with justification, one center that should have primary jurisdiction over a proposed combination product. This is typically the center that would govern the "primary mode of action" of the product, or the center that has the precedent of governing prior related products. Such a request should be discussed with that center prior to submission of the request. This is done either as a request for designation (RFD) or in the premarket application (PMA) itself. The OCP then makes a final decision, due within 60 days.

Products that are classified primarily as a device may face less burdensome review and lower costs, but conversely would not receive the potential FDA market protections that drug classification might allow. So in one example, a dual product could be primarily classified as a device, and then a drug or biologic agent on the device would be assigned to the CDER or CBER (and any previously unapproved agent may also need to be registered with the U.S. Pharmacopeia in a draft monograph). Also of note, biologics agents could theoretically be assigned for review either through the device pathway (using appropriate IDE/PMN/PMA applications) or through the drug pathway (using appropriate IND/NDA applications), whichever is most appropriate as determined by the FDA. In certain cases where the line is unclear, the decision can turn on whether the biologic agent is metabolized or whether it is used for a structural, functional, or diagnostic purpose. The FDA provides further guidance for industry entitled, "How to Write a Request for Designation" at http://www.fda.gov/RegulatoryInformation/Guidances/ucm126053.htm.

Healthcare Reimbursement

In any healthcare technology, reimbursement is an essential issue because the product must fit into a tightly controlled reimbursement system. As a brief overview of healthcare reimbursement, all medical, surgical, and diagnostic services are assigned a reimbursement code. The codes account for not just the treatment but also the setting, the concurrent conditions of the patient (comorbidities), and many other details of the physician assessment and therapeutic intervention (including depth of assessment, complexity of the treatment, products used for the treatment, and/or complications).

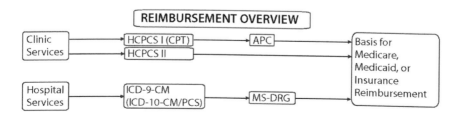

111

For historical reasons, coding systems are different between hospital and clinic settings. ICD-9-CM codes are those that cover hospital (inpatient) services, and HCPCS codes are those that cover treatments in office settings (outpatient). The HCPCS codes cover outpatient physician services (HCPCS I codes, normally called CPT codes by physicians, or CDT codes by dentists), as well as equipment purchased and used by the patient outside the treatment setting (HCPCS II codes).

Physicians working in the outpatient setting thus charge for exams, diagnostics, and treatments via CPT codes. Similarly, dentists charges for exams, diagnostics, and procedures through CDT codes (also called ADA codes). For dentistry, however, Medicare will only cover dental procedures related to medical conditions, such as cancer, heart disease, & trauma.

When a patient receives a treatment, reimbursement requests are made both for the physician and the facility. ICD-9-CM codes for inpatient treatments are actually translated into "MS-DRG" groups (which classify services by severity of the diagnosis), and HCPCS codes are actually translated into "APC" codes. APC and MS-DRG reimbursement rates change each year.

Of note, in 2013, the ICD-9-CM codes will be replaced by the split ICD-10 coding system: ICD-10-CM codes for diagnoses and the ICD-10-PCS codes for procedures. There are multiple reasons for the change, including updating codes for advances in technology, ability to document adverse events and iatrogenic complications, integration with electronic medical records, and simply running out of room for new ICD-9 codes.

Codes are assigned relative value units (RVUs), essentially based on both physician involvement and facility and administrative (F&A) costs. The RVUs are then converted to a reimbursement amount based on an annual conversion factor and the geographic location. RVUs do not necessarily correspond to difficulty or time given by the physician, varying to a notable degree among medical specialties.

Devices may be covered as part of existing CPT or ICD-9-CM codes, but devices are also often documented as a "C-code." Each device can be assigned a C-code, and the Centers for Medicare & Medicaid Services (CMS) may assign new C-codes to new devices, and each clinical use of the device is documented using the C-code. C-codes may be given to new technologies, thereby allowing a possible temporary reimbursement method, but many C-codes are not reimbursed directly but rather used to calculate resource costs and bundle reimbursement rates.

In cases where reimbursement for a new technology is not adequate or appropriate under current codes, the process for requesting new codes or a change in current coding is carried out through the CMS for all C-codes, APC codes, MS-DRG codes, and ICD-9/10 codes, and through the American Medical Association (AMA) for CPT codes. For the CMS, a code revision package, called an "addendum," must be completed and submitted at least two months prior to the annual CMS coordination and maintenance meeting. The addendum should include an explanation of the inadequacy of the current system, a description of the new treatment and its benefits, and how the new treatment should be coded. This requires significant evidence that the treatment is substantially beneficial, considering that every new reimbursement essentially shifts money away from current treatments. Open comments are then allowed on the suggestion, and a decision is later made, which, if changed, would take effect the following year. The company will likely also need to negotiate a national coverage determination for the code through CMS. More information on the code revision package can be found at https://www.cms.gov/ICD9ProviderDiagnosticCodes/02_newrevisedcodes.asp

A "CPT III" code is a code that may be allowed for a new technology before a formal CPT code is assigned, but a CPT III code does not permit reimbursement, only documentation of use. The CPT III code is often requested along with a request through CMS for a new APC code, and the sponsor must then also lobby for local coverage determinations determined by CMS. Therefore, before approval of new formal CPT or ICD codes, a C-code or CPT III code may sometimes be used in conjunction with a standard CPT or ICD code (where the CPT or ICD code describes the treatment, or if no current CPT or ICD code adequately describes the treatment, then a miscellaneous category of CPT or ICD code within the particular specialty may be used). The CPT and APC code request process must usually be submitted by a physician specialty society lobbying on behalf of the company. More information on CPT requests can be found at http://www.ama-assn.org/ama/pub/physician-resources/solutions-managing-your-practice/coding-billing-insurance/cpt/applying-cpt-codes.page.

The decision of whether a new technology will be reimbursed through CMS and insurance does not just depend on scientific merit and regulatory approval of the technology, but also many other factors, such as whether the technology provides meaningfully better care than current therapies, easier or faster treatment protocols, lower costs, greater safety, lower error or malpractice risks, and/or physician-patient demand. Healthcare providers and administrators must therefore decide whether the technology is something worth integrating into their practice, usually based on the factors above, and must then support the product or service for reimbursement. Unfortunately, however, sometimes the difficulty of adapting to new technologies can appear more burdensome than the less distinct difficulties of sticking with a status quo, causing just one of many potential barriers to entry.

§

PART V – TAX & ACCOUNTING

"Time is but the stream I go a-fishing in.
I drink at it; but while I drink
I see the sandy bottom and detect how shallow it is.
Its thin current slides away, but eternity remains."
Henry David Thoreau, *Walden*

"Science is a wonderful thing
if one does not have to earn one's living at it."
Albert Einstein, *Draft Letter 1951*

"Money often costs too much."
Ralph Waldo Emerson, *The Conduct of Life (VI:III)*

Taxes

This chapter is intended to be somewhat concise, as tax and accounting information could take volumes. The information included here is meant simply as an overview of the more likely aspects that an entrepreneur will need to understand, and these topics can be researched in more detail according to specific circumstances. Some aspects of taxes and accounting were also briefly touched upon in other sections, such as pass-through taxation status and implications of equity ownership in the first section. None of this information should be construed as legal tax or accounting advice.

It is important to determine current tax laws at the federal, state, and local levels. Many business structures, including a sole proprietorship, partnership, and LLC, have *pass-through* or *disregard* tax status, which passes any profits or losses through the company to its owners and allows the company's tax filings to be submitted as part of the owner's tax filings. This allows the company's profits to essentially count as salary of the owner(s), thus avoiding double taxing both the company and the individual.

The IRS, however, does not allow pass-through taxation for standard corporations (C-corps). If desired, an LLC or partnership can be converted into corporate status for tax purposes (using IRS form 8832), or even converted to an official C-corporation by changing registration with the state. However, once this is done the company cannot convert back to the pass-through or disregard status; conversion of a corporation to an LLC would essentially warrant taxation of all company assets in the process. A corporation can, however, elect pass-through status by filing IRS form 2553 to elect S-corporation status, but there are other important issues to understand if considering this.

Equity compensation such as stock options and various types of stock awards can be offered to board members, officers, and employees. There are many complex rules and regulations for all types of equity compensation—for example, board members and executives generally cannot profit by selling their equity shares within six months of acquiring them. Corporations can sometimes allow certain payments of dividends or equity compensation or awards with deferred taxation, whereas an LLC pass-through status means that equity, grants, options, or dividend compensation will typically be counted as personal income and the value subject to income and/or capital gains taxes in that same tax period, even if no money is actually paid. This means that ownership in the company may create tax obligations even when no compensation is physically received. Many companies of both structure-types use stock options, restricted stock awards, stock purchase plans, and/or preferred shares with liquidation preferences that can sometimes allow delayed, deferred, or reduced tax obligations. More details on equity considerations can be found in the *Company Structure* and *Investment Capital* sections. Any equity compensation plans should be made with careful legal and financial guidance.

Depending on the location of the business, there may be state, city, and/or county taxation. Some states have adopted flat corporate tax rates, although sales and use tax will often be levied at both the state and local level. Local taxes may include gross receipts tax, real estate taxes, tangible property taxes, inventory taxes, utility taxes, license taxes, excise taxes, consumer taxes, and machinery and tools taxes. Locales may also implement peculiar and transient tax credits to attract employers to the area (e.g., job credits, worker retraining credits, relocation credits, etc.). Companies must generally pay taxes on both domestic and international profits, although some companies have established a parent company (sometimes just an office) in a foreign country with favorable tax laws in order to circumvent domestic tax payments.

When businesses have employees, various payroll withholdings may apply, including federal income tax (as detailed in Publication 15), state income tax, social security tax (6.2%, up to the max amount of $6,622, based on a cap of $106,800 subject to the tax), Medicare tax (1.45%, up to the max amount of $1,549, again based on a cap of $106,800 subject to the tax), state income tax, local withholdings, and disability and unemployment taxes (FUTA and SUTA). Using payroll software, contracting these services, or hiring an accounting assistant can save much time and effort.

In addition, employer and employees split the costs of social security and Medicare taxes, paying a total of 15.3% (6.2% each for social security and 1.45% each for Medicare, with no more than $106,800 subject to these taxes). The temporary 2011-2012 payroll tax cut lowers the 6.2% payment to 4.2% for the employee only, and, if self-employed, lowers the overall rate from 15.3% to 10.4% (again, with a maximum $106,800 subject to the tax rate). In addition to employee withholdings mentioned above, there may be voluntary payroll deductions such as health insurance, retirement savings, or employee stock purchase plans, which may qualify to be paid as either "pre-tax" or "post-tax."

Some corporations and LLCs (particularly those with pass-through tax status) can choose to file annually rather than quarterly, but larger entities are typically required to file quarterly. For state taxes, some states may also require some businesses to file quarterly returns rather than annual returns, depending on the structure and nature of the business.

The company's federal tax returns may need to include either Form 941 (quarterly return) or Form 944 (annual return). Other IRS forms for companies with employees may include Form 940 (FUTA), Form 945 (federal income tax withheld from non-payroll payments), Form 1099, and W-2 statements. Any independent contract worker who was paid $600 or more in the year should be provided with a 1099MISC form. The state regulates what companies must provide unemployment insurance (usually based on duration, salary, or full-time status of a worker's employment), and the state also regulates what companies are required to purchase worker's compensation insurance (usually based on the number of employees in the company).

When filing business earnings with the standard personal Form 1040 filing, business earnings should be reported on either a Schedule SE (for self-employed), Schedule C for sole proprietorship or single-member LLC, Schedule E for multi-member LLCs and S-corporations, or Schedule F for farming. Form 1065 (Schedule K-1) must be filed annually by each member of a partnership to inform the IRS of the status of the partnership and individual earnings. The IRS website lists pertinent forms for LLCs at http://www.irs.gov/businesses/small/article/0,,id=158448,00.html and for corporations at http://www.irs.gov/businesses/corporations/index.html.

Equipment and tangible assets that are intended for long-term use by the company (typically >1 year) may be considered "capital assets" and allowed "depreciation deductions." This typically includes office furniture, tools, machinery, appliances, equipment, and can even include computer software, patents, and exclusive patent licenses. Capital assets can be treated differently than general expenses using depreciation deductions that allow the expense of the asset to be divided over a certain number of years (e.g., 30 years for a vehicle, 5 years for farm equipment, 3-5 years for a computer, etc.). Tax deductions may be made based on the asset's value divided by the prescribed number of years. So for example, a $3000 computer could be deducted as an expense at $1000 per year for 3 years. MACRS depreciation tables are freely available online or with tax software for searching depreciation asset class and life for recovery.

Rather than standard depreciation rules, capital assets can sometimes be written off entirely in one year. In the 2010-2011 tax years at least, a 100% first-year depreciation bonus was allowed, meaning that capital asset costs could be written off immediately (at least on most assets that would otherwise depreciate over 20 years or less). Many capital expenditures are written off immediately by using the "Section 179" deduction (with maximum write-off limits changing each year, at $500,000 in 2011). If a company is not yet profitable, however, it may actually be worth using depreciation to create future tax deductions for when the company is profitable. Supplies and materials are expenses that can typically be deducted directly from earnings for tax purposes.

Depending on the state, many items of equipment may be sales tax exempt, including items for resale or materials and machinery for manufacturing. The details of state tax exemptions are usually provided in state tax exemption forms. Also of note, businesses can usually carry forward net operating losses from the previous 2-5 years (again, check updated tax laws).

R&D costs may also be eligible for tax exemptions (it is not yet clear if the R&D tax credit will extend beyond the 2011 tax year), and sometimes there are even tax grants available through the IRS itself, but these tax grants change year to year and tend to have very particular criteria for the type and purpose of the work being done by the company. Some examples include the Orphan Drug Credit (see Form 8820), Renewable Energy Credit (see Form 8835), Biodiesel and Renewable Fuel (see Form 8864), Carbon Dioxide Sequestration Credit (see Form 8933), or Qualifying Advanced Energy Project or Qualifying Therapeutic Discovery Project Credit.

Accounting

For a startup company, it is perfectly acceptable to keep track of expenses in an Excel spreadsheet on a *cash basis* (which works just like a standard checking account, keeping track of all expenses and earnings). However, as billing and expenses become more complex, and as you hire employees, business accounting software can aid significantly in this work. Many forms of accounting and payroll software systems are available; perhaps the most widely used system for small businesses is Quickbooks, which is relatively inexpensive and can perform the necessary functions for most small companies, including creating profit and loss statements, balance sheets, accounts receivable, accounts payable, invoice statements, etc. This system also allows *accrual basis* accounting, which is the standard for most larger companies, especially companies that will be obtaining investment financing (accrual basis is similar to cash basis, but also includes future known expenses and revenue that may not yet show up in a checking account, such as future payment obligations to employees, incoming invoices, grant contracts, or debt obligations).

It should be noted that both methods, cash basis and accrual basis, are discussed here as a single-entry bookkeeping system, which is the standard system used for many small businesses due to simplicity. A single-entry system is essentially a method to show a running balance of one account, or one ledger, like a checking account. A double-entry system is more complex and is typically run by a professional bookkeeper. The double-entry system uses multiple ledgers, comparing the sum of debits with the sum of credits for all accounts. The ledgers may include a sales ledger, a purchase ledger, and a general ledger. The general ledger combines revenue and expenses with capital, assets, and liabilities. Every time money is gained or lost, it is considered to simultaneously credit one account and debit another, making a "zero-sum" function. By assigning balancing credits and debits to every account, this system enables a double-check against clerical error and fraud.

Of note, a ledger may also utilize a separate "daybook" or "journal" to record individual transactions, which can then be added *en bloc* back into the ledger. The operating principle for double-entry bookkeeping is that the total assets of a company, minus its liabilities, should equal its capital. Conveniently, Quickbooks can run either a single-entry or a double-entry system of accounting. If documenting finances in your own spreadsheets, categorizing expenses and revenue can help speed up tax processing. In particular, you should categorize equipment and capital assets, fees paid for services, insurance costs, interest payments, office and facility expenses, repairs and maintenance, payroll expenses, utilities, tax payments, advertising costs, and business travel expenses (including mileage logs for vehicle deductions).

For accounting, it will also be helpful to review the information under the previous *Budget & Accounting* section under *Grants*, even if not using grants. Be aware that for SBIR/STTR grants or other federal funding, you will need to keep costs segregated into Direct, Indirect, or Unallowable categories, as explained in the *SBIR/STTR Grants* section. Accomplishing this in Quickbooks may require other add-on modules, so some businesses choose to simply document it in their own data entry software format. Finally, it is important to not co-mingle business funds and personal funds, since this can create accounting confusion and can erode the limited liability protection provided to the company.

APPENDIX I
STATE BUSINESS REGISTRATION

[Visit http://www.innovatorguide.com/guide.html for live links]

Alabama	http://sos.alabama.gov/BusinessServices/
Alaska	http://commerce.alaska.gov/occ/
Arizona	http://www.azsos.gov/business_services/filings.htm
Arkansas	http://www.sos.arkansas.gov/BCS/Pages/default.aspx
California	http://www.sos.ca.gov/business/forms.htm
Colorado	http://www.sos.state.co.us/pubs/BusinessAndLicensing/
Connecticut	https://drsbustax.ct.gov/REG/REGISTRATION.ASPX
Delaware	https://onestop.delaware.gov/osbrlpublic/
District of Columbia	http://brc.dc.gov/licenses/licenses.asp
Florida	http://www.stateofflorida.com/doinbusinfla.html
Georgia	http://www.sos.ga.gov/corporations/
Hawaii	http://hawaii.gov/dcca/breg
Idaho	http://business.idaho.gov/
Illinois	http://tax.illinois.gov/Businesses/register.htm
Indiana	http://www.in.gov/dor/3744.htm
Iowa	http://www.iowa.gov/tax/business/newbus.html
Kansas	https://www.kansas.gov/businesscenter/index.html
Kentucky	http://revenue.ky.gov/business/register.htm
Louisiana	http://rev.louisiana.gov/sections/business/intro.aspx
Maine	http://www.maine.gov/portal/business/licensing.html
Maryland	http://www.dat.state.md.us/sdatweb/checklist.html
Massachusetts	http://www.mass.gov/portal/business/
Michigan	http://www.michigan.gov/business
Minnesota	http://www.sos.state.mn.us/index.aspx?page=92
Mississippi	http://www.sos.ms.gov/business_services.aspx
Missouri	http://www.business.mo.gov/
Montana	http://sos.mt.gov/Business/Forms/
Nebraska	https://www.nebraska.gov/osbr/index.cgi
Nevada	http://nvsos.gov/index.aspx?page=419
New Hampshire	http://www.revenue.nh.gov/business/index.htm
New Jersey	http://www.state.nj.us/njbusiness/registration/
New Mexico	http://www.tax.newmexico.gov/Businesses/
New York	http://www.dos.ny.gov/corps/
North Carolina	http://www.secretary.state.nc.us/corporations/
North Dakota	http://www.nd.gov/businessreg/
Ohio	http://business.ohio.gov/
Oklahoma	https://www.sos.ok.gov/corp/filing.aspx

Oregon	http://www.filinginoregon.com/pages/business_registry/
Pennsylvania	http://www.paopen4business.state.pa.us/
Rhode Island	http://www.ri.gov/business/
South Carolina	https://www.scbos.sc.gov/
South Dakota	http://sdsos.gov/business/Default.aspx
Tennessee	http://www.tn.gov/topics/Business
Texas	http://www.sos.state.tx.us/corp/index.shtml
Utah	http://osbr.utah.gov/
Vermont	http://corps.sec.state.vt.us/
Virginia	http://www.tax.virginia.gov/business/
Virgin Islands	http://dlca.vi.gov/businesslicense/
Washington	http://bls.dor.wa.gov/startbusiness.aspx
West Virginia	http://www.business4wv.com/
Wisconsin	http://www.wisconsin.gov/state/byb/name.html
Wyoming	http://soswy.state.wy.us/Business/Business.aspx

APPENDIX II
EXAMPLE OF ARTICLES OF
ORGANIZATION/OPERATING AGREEMENT

The name of the company is hereby declared to be _name of company_. _Name of company_ was officially founded and registered in the state of _state_ on _date_ as a _structure (e.g., limited liability company)_. The company's official operating location and state license registration will be _address_. Its members comprise _name(s)_, who own(s) and operate(s) the company. The _president/chief member/chief executive/etc._ is _name(s)...._ This signifies that _name(s)_ owns and operates the company's assets, powers, rights, responsibilities, and all other functionalities, and that _name(s)_ has invested the time, effort, materials, and financial contributions that have created _name of company_. The company may engage in any and all lawful activities and legal business permitted under the laws of the United States.

The assets, powers, rights, responsibilities, and ownership may be appropriated as necessary solely by majority vote of the member(s), and shall be done with formal and binding legal agreements. Each member's voting power shall be directly proportionate to his or her share ownership in the company. Further members may be added only by approval of majority vote of current members. Percentage of ownership in the company may not correspond to each member's capital contribution or proportion of capital investment in the company; in other words, ownership in the company is not a function of capital, time, or assets contributed, but rather, a pre-agreed upon proportion of membership shares as offered by the company. All proprietary knowledge, rights, and technology remain property of the company; additional non-disclosure agreements and/or non-compete agreements may also be required of the members.

A general meeting of the company shall be held at the end of each fiscal year, where any member may request a vote on any issue. Additional meetings may also be held at the request of any member, or by someone who has been granted the authority by the members to convene such meetings. Majority vote shall be the final decision in all cases. In the case of a tie, _name(s)_ shall be the final decision maker.

For financial accounting and tax purposes, net profits or net losses will be determined on an annual basis or as required by federal and/or state requirements, and all profits and losses shall be considered the property of the company. If the company earns profit but has reinvested the profit or otherwise deferred compensation to members, the company may choose by majority vote to compensate its members enough to cover any consequent income tax responsibilities based on their allocated investiture in the company. Regarding distribution of profits, there will be no requirement to distribute profits or pay dividends to any owners, investors, or employees unless authorized by the majority of members, or as agreed upon in separate legal contracts, or as required by law. Bonuses or compensation from company profits (distributive shares) shall be proportionate to each member's ownership in the company, unless otherwise decided by majority vote of members and dictated in legal agreement of special allocation. In the infancy and establishment of *name of company,* it is recognized that there may be no net profit, and all earnings may be re-invested into the company until otherwise deemed appropriate by the members. All other payments, salaries, bonuses, rewards, and compensation shall be purely at the discretion of *name(s),* or at the discretion of the majority vote of members, or according to separate legal agreements and contracts.

It is set forth that the number of shares of stock in *name of company* is *number of shares*. *Name(s)* owns *number of shares*.... Any transfer or sale of ownership, assets, powers, rights, responsibilities, and financial stake may only be done when authorized by majority vote of all members. If the company is sold, compensation shall be distributed to members proportionate to their percentage ownership in the company and according to written agreements and contracts. If members do not adequately fulfill their duties and obligations, or if they act in a manner that damages the company and its success, such owners may be stripped of their ownership and voting rights by majority vote of all members and compensated according to legal requirements. If a member dies or becomes permanently disabled, such member's share ownership may be reclaimed by the company and fair market value of such shares shall be compensated to the member or the member's next of kin. These articles of organization may be amended as necessary only as approved by majority vote of all members. The undersigned certify that they execute these articles under oath for the purposes stated above.

APPENDIX III
BUSINESS PLAN

Coversheet

Executive Summary (see *Executive Summary* section)

Table of Contents

Business Plan:

I. The Company
    a. Description of Business
    b. Product or Service
        i. Overview
        ii. Customer Need & Significance
        iii. Company Solution & Value Proposition
        iv. Competition & Feasibility Analysis
        v. Reimbursement
        vi. Intellectual Property & Strategy
        vii. Supporting Data
        viii. Animal/Human Studies
        ix. Regulatory Strategy
        x. Summary of Critical Milestones
        xi. Risk Analysis
    c. Operating Procedures & Policies
    d. Founders/Accomplishments/Expertise
    e. Other Personnel
    f. Location & Licenses

II. Market & Financial Data
    a. Market Analysis & Strategy
    b. Overview of Requested Funding
        i. Funding Requirements
        ii. Purpose of Equity Capital
    c. Overview of Current Funding
        i. Grants and Research Funding
        ii. Loan Applications and Amounts
        iii. Credit Availability
        iv. Private Equity/Financing Round
        v. Current Revenue

d. Equipment and Supply List

e. Balance Sheet

    i. Assets/Equity

    ii. Capital

    iii. Liabilities

f. Prior Earnings (GAAP standards)

g. Return on Investment Analysis

h. Projected Earnings and Cash Flow

    i. 3-10 Year Annual Summary (Revenue + Profit/EBITDA)

    ii. Capital Expenditures

    iii. R&D Expenses

    iv. Materials/Supplies Expenses

    v. Manufacturing Expenses

    vi. Facilities Expenses

    vii. Administrative Expenses

    viii. Staffing Expenses

    ix. Operating Expenses

    x. Intellectual Property Expenses

    xi. Regulatory Approval Expenses

    xii. Animal/Human Studies Expenses

    xiii. Sales & Distribution Expenses

    xiv. Debt Financing

    xv. Sales and Consulting Revenue

    xvi. Licensing Revenue

    xvii. Grant Revenue

    xviii. Strategic Partnership Revenue

i. Anticipated Exit Strategy

III. Additional Documentation

a. Financial Statement of Principals

b. Copy of Resumes/CVs of Principals

c. Copy of Licenses and Legal Documentation

d. Copy of Patent Documentation

e. Proposed Lease for Building Space

f. Copy of Letter of Intent from Contractors & Manufacturers

g. Copy of Prior Research and Publications

h. Endorsements from Experts in the Field

APPENDIX IV
CLINICAL PROTOCOL OUTLINE

<u>Title Page</u>
Title of Study
Protocol Reference Number/Version Number
Date
Principal Investigator/Group Chair
Name of Sponsor Organization
Contact Information
Partnering Institutions/Cooperative Groups

<u>Introduction and Background</u>
Introduction
Background
Rationale
Relevant Prior Studies (pre-clinical/clinical, published/unpublished)
Literature Review
Summary of Epidemiologic Data
Potential Benefits
Potential Risks

<u>Purpose and Objectives</u>
Purpose
Objectives (Primary/Secondary)
Hypotheses
Justification (Devices)
Planned Observations/Measurements
Study Design
        Phase I: Outline and Overview of Investigation
        Phase II-III: Detailed Descriptions of Investigations

<u>Pharmaceutical Information</u>
PDS name/number
Dosage Forms
Indications
Contraindications

Interactive Substances

Precautions

Ingredients

Drug chemical composition and stability

Excipient formulation

Manufacturing

Packaging

Labeling

Preparation

Storage Requirements

Batch Analysis & GMP Compliance

Dosing Specifications and Justification

    Dosing Schedule

    Route of Administration

    Body Weight Basis

    Duration/Cycle/Treatment Period

    Administration Instructions

    Total Dose/Maximum Dose

Device Information

Principles of Operation

Intended Purpose

Manufacture Details

Model/Type

Labeling

Components

Intended Indications

Materials Contacting Human Tissue and Fluids

Training and Experience Required for Device Operation

Description of Specific Medical/Surgical Procedures of Use

Number of Devices to Be Used

Exposure and Duration of Use of Device

Analysis of Biocompatibility (ISO10993)

Comparison of Other Similar Devices

Information Security of Device (Confidentiality, Integrity, Availability, and Accountability)

Description of other devices or medications to be used in the study

Lot Analysis & GMP Compliance

Traceability
Estimated Enrollment Time
Adverse Effects, Contraindications, Hazards, Interference Conditions, Warnings, Precautions

Treatment Plan and Procedures
Statement of Adherence to GLP/GMP/GCP
Statement of Adherence to Protocol Design, Ethical Conduct, and Federal Regulatory Requirements
Overall Study Design
Study Flow Chart
Study Duration
Schedule of Events
Controls (Treated v. Untreated, Placebo Controlled, Standard of Care Comparison, Historical Control, Prospective Randomized Controlled, Etc.)
Intended Treatment Population
Selection of Control Group
Patient Eligibility (inclusion/exclusion criteria, including any age, sex, conditions, screening visit)
Accessory Baseline Data (concurrent meds, family history, social history, etc.)
Method of Subject Selection
Randomization/Allocation/Coding/Decoding Procedures
Description of All Subject Treatments, Procedures, Lab Tests, Normal Ranges & Parameters
Monitoring of Subjects
Methods of Avoiding Bias/Analysis of Confounding Variables/Patient Compliance
Protocols for Breaking Randomization/Blinding
Pregnancy Reporting
Participating Study Centers
Investigators and Sub-Investigators
Safety Assessments (Definition of parameters, methods, timing, etc.)
Risk Analysis (known and potential risks)/Methods of Minimizing Risks
Definition of Adverse Events/Serious Adverse Events (Pharmaceutical)
Definition of Adverse Device Effects/Device Deficiencies (Device)
Protocols for Adverse Event Timely Reporting, Recording, and Follow-up
Laboratory Anomalies as Adverse Events
Emergency Contact Information

Methods and Equipment for Observations and Data Collection/Validation
Concomitant Treatments (Permitted/Prohibited)
Rescue Treatments
Dose Modification for Adverse Events
Criteria for Response Assessment
Duration of Subject Participation
Patient Follow-up (unscheduled visits, end-of-study visit, post-study visits)
Monitoring (Devices)
Identification of Local Tissue Reactions (Devices)
Study Supplies
Outcome Measures/Primary and Secondary Endpoints/Surrogate Endpoints
Number of Subjects Involved in Study
Withdrawal of Subjects
Criteria for Discontinuation or Replacement of Individual Subjects
Criteria for Study Termination
Procedure for Protocol Deviations
Preventative Corrective Protocols/Notification Requirements
Disqualification of Investigators

Statistical Methods
Statistical Design and Protocols
Level of Significance
Randomization/Subject Allocation
Primary/Secondary/Surrogate Endpoints
Subgroup Analysis
Data Parameters and Capture Methods
Total Sample Size (justified for primary and secondary outcome measures/power analysis)
Sample Size at Each Study Site (Multicenter Studies)
Type I and II Errors
Comparative Study Targets
Assessment of Efficacy for Endpoints
Significance Levels and Confidence Intervals
Study Duration Rationale
Expected Drop-out Rates
Pass/fail criteria (Devices)
Interim Analysis Protocols
Study Termination Protocols

Outcome Parameters
Primary and Secondary Endpoints
Subgroup Analysis
Quality Control and Data Handling
Preliminary Financial/Economic/Cost-Benefit Analysis

Records
Protection of Patient Confidentiality
Signed Protocols (with Amendments & Revisions)
Data Handling and Record Keeping
Data Security and Integrity
Patient Informed Consent Forms
Records of Retained Tissue Samples
Patient Characteristics and Eligibility Data/ Screening Forms
Patient Clinical Information/Enrollment Lists
Patient Code List
Research Forms (for surgery, pathology, laboratory, radiology, etc.)
Investigators Summaries
Treating Physician Summaries
Regulatory Authority Approvals
Auditing Certificates
IRB Annual Updates
All Communications (FDA, Sponsor, CRO, Investigators, Institutions, etc.)

Participation
Executive Committee (typically a senior clinical investigator, a company representative, a CRO representative, etc.)
Study Administration
Participating Centers and Responsibilities
Research and Laboratory Facilities
Participating Healthcare Professionals and Responsibilities
Data Safety Monitoring Board (for pivotal and phase II/III studies)
Ethical Considerations and Principles
Use of Information
Financial Disclosure
Insurance Statement
Signed Agreements & Contracts (CRO, Sponsor, Investigators, Institutions, etc.)

Publication and Reporting Policy

References

Investigator's Signature

Forms

Investigator's Brochure

Informed Consent Forms

Advertisements for Subject Recruitment

Information Provided to Subjects

APPENDIX V
INVESTIGATIONAL DEVICE EXEMPTION (IDE) OUTLINE

Submitter Name and Contact Details
Brief Overview of Clinical Plan

> Descriptive Title
> Study Design
> Type of Controls
> Sample Size
> Outcome Measures

Summary of Prior Data

> Prior Laboratory Testing
> Prior Animal Studies
> Prior Clinical Studies
> Review of Relevant Literature
> Review of Unpublished Information
> Summary of All Adverse Outcomes
> Statement of Compliance with GLP/GMP/GCP.
> Batch/Lot Analysis & Compliance
> References (with copies)

Clinical Study Protocol

> Description of the Device
> Objectives
> Indications
> Study Design and Methodology
> Monitoring Procedures
> Labeling
> Duration
> Primary (& Secondary) Outcome Measures
> Sample Size
> Type of Controls (Treated v. Untreated, Placebo Controlled, Standard of Care Comparison, Historical Control, Prospective Randomized Controlled, Etc.)
> Risk Analysis
> Informed Consent
> Database and Records

Statement to comply with annual progress reports, 30-day reports of defective devices, and reports of adverse effects.

(May also need to include other aspects included in Appendix IV)

Device Labeling

Manufacturer Info

Packager Info

Sterilization Info

Quantity of Package Contents

Statement: "CAUTION – For Investigational Use Only" (or for diagnostic devices: "For Research Use Only: The performance characteristics of this product have not been established.")

Statement that the device will not claim to be safe or effective for the indications

Contraindications, Hazards, Adverse Effects, Interference Conditions, Warnings, Precautions

Quality Systems Controls (QS/GMP)

List and Certification of All Investigators

IRB Approval and Contact Information

Statement that applicant will maintain IRB approvals at all study sites

Informed Consent Forms

Institutions Involved in the Study and Contact Information

Statement that FDA will be notified of any changes in plan or protocol

Statement of whether the device will be charged to the patient and if so, justification for why it should not be considered commercialization.

Any additional information that the FDA requests

APPENDIX VI
510(K) OUTLINE

Submit as bound volume(s), 8.5x11 inch paper, with two duplicate copies. The order of sections may be rearranged except for the cover sheets. See 21 CFR part 807 subpart E for all rules on 510(k) submissions, and also the guidance on the FDA website at: http://www.fda.gov/MedicalDevices/DeviceRegulationandGuidance/Guidance Documents/ucm084365.htm

"Medical Device User Fee Cover Sheet" (MDUFMA) FDA Form 3601
"CDRH Premarket Review Submission Cover Sheet"
"510(k) Submission" cover letter ("Executive Summary")
    Submission Date
    Applicant name and full contact information
    Primary contact information for FDA communication
    Establishment Registration Number (or statement that the establishment will be registered within 30 days of market approval.)
    Common Name of Device
    Trade Name of Device
    Device Classification (or statement that the FDA has not yet registered such a device and applicant's suggested assignment of classification and product code)
    Design and Use
        Indication
        Prescription or OTC
        Inclusion of any tissue or biologic products
        Inclusion of any drug or biologic agents
        Whether the device must be sterile
        Whether the device is implanted
    Explanation of 510(k) Pathway
        New device, modified device, end-user device, or unfinished component
        New indications for use or new device design
        510(k) Numbers for Prior Applications and Related Devices

Specific Predicate Devices and 510(k) Numbers, Product
Codes, Trade Names, and Registration Numbers of
Manufacturers and Contracted Sterilizers and Packagers.
Identification of any reprocessed single-use devices or
exempt devices that may no longer meet exemption
qualifications

Compliance with product controls and performance standards (e.g.,
FD&C section 513-514, RCHSA, 21 CFR 800-1000, or a statement that
no consensus standards or controls exist).

Any prior FDA communication with documentation numbers

Table of Contents

510(k) Screening Checklist (to verify inclusion of all required elements)

Introduction

General Information

Name of Device

Classification (according to FD&C section 513)

Compliance with Performance Standards (according to FD&C section
514)

Indications for Use

510(k) Summary or Statement (see 21 CFR 807.92 or 807.93)

Class III Certification and Summary of Risks (see 21 CFR 807.94)

Statement of Truth and Accuracy

Financial Statement and Disclosure (FDA Forms 3454 and 3455)

Labeling

Description

Intended Use

Directions for Use

Photographs

Engineering Drawings

Specifications

Bench-top, animal, and/or clinical testing

Sterilization

Shelf life

Biocompatibility

Software

Electrical Safety/Electromagnetic Compatibility (see CDRH
Compatibility Program and IEC 60601-1)

Substantial Equivalence Comparison

Description and Discussion (Indications, Technology, Performance)
    Indications
    Target Population
    Anatomical Sites
    Facilities where used
    Energy used or delivered
    Human factors
    Design
    Materials
    Biocompatibility
    Environment/Disposal Issues
    Sterility
    Electrical/Mechanical/Chemical/Thermal/Radiation Safety
Predicate Devices
Supporting Data (clinical and non-clinical)
Declaration of Conformity
    Consensus Standards
    Statement of each standard that was met or not met
    Statement of adaptations or modifications for each standard
    Statement of standards not applicable to the device
    Statement of any deviations from standards
    Statement of any differences between tested device and
    expected marketed device
    Contact information for testing lab and certifying authority
    Reference to "Recognition and Use of Consensus Standards"
Performance
    Bench-Top Testing Data
    Animal Testing Data
    Clinical Testing Data
Certification of Product Kit Components
Any Additional Requirements (e.g., Risk Analysis, Manufacturing, etc.)

APPENDIX VII
INCUBATORS & ACCELERATORS

Y Combinator
Mountain View, CA
http://ycombinator.com/

I/O Ventures
San Francisco, CA
http://www.ventures.io/

Kicklabs
San Francisco, CA
http://www.kicklabs.com/

Menlo Park Incubator
Menlo Park, CA
http://www.menloincubator.com/

The Pfizer Incubator
San Diego, CA
http://www.thepfizerincubator.com

SD Technology Incubator
San Diego, CA
http://www.sdincubator.org

SD Science Center
San Diego, CA
http://www.sdsciencecenter.com/

CCAT
San Diego, CA
http://www.ccatsandiego.org/aboutus.html

CONNECT
San Diego, CA
http://www.connect.org

BioCom
San Diego, CA
http://www.biocom.org

BioInnovations Gateway
Salt Lake City, UT
http://www.innovationutah.com/BiG.html

Wayne Brown Institute
Salt Lake City, UT
http://www.venturecapital.org/

Utah Research Park
Salt Lake City, UT
http://www.research.utah.edu/econ/

BoomStartup
Salt Lake City, UT
http://www.boomstartup.com/

USTAR
Salt Lake City, UT
http://www.innovationutah.com/

Fitzsimmons Life Science Campus
Aurora, CO
http://fitzscience.com/

TechStars
Boulder, CO
http://www.techstars.com/

Microsoft Kinect
Seattle, WA
http://www.microsoft.com/bizspark/kinectaccelerator/

8ninths
Seattle, WA
http://www.8ninths.com/

TechStars
Seattle, WA
http://www.techstars.com/

ONAMI
Corvallis, OR
http://onami.us/

Tech Wildcatters
Dallas, TX
http://techwildcatters.com/

Capital Factory
Austin, TX
http://www.capitalfactory.com/

TechStars
San Antonio, TX
http://www.techstars.com/

Science Foundation AZ
Phoenix, AZ
http://www.sfaz.org/

TechStars
New York City, NY
http://www.techstars.com/

NYC SeedStart
New York, NY
http://www.nycseedstart.com/

RIT Entrepeneurs Hall
Rochester, NY
http://www.rit.edu/research/simonecenter/

TechStars
Boston, MA
http://www.techstars.com/

DreamIt Ventures
Philadelphia, PA
http://dreamitventures.com/

AlphaLab
Pittsburgh, PA
http://www.alphalab.org/

JumpStart
Cleveland, OH
http://www.jumpstartinc.org/

The Brandery
Cincinnati, OH
http://brandery.org/

LaunchHouse
Shaker Heights, OH
http://launchhouse.com/

TechTown
Detroit, MI
http://techtownwsu.org/

MTA
Ridgeland, MI
http://www.technologyalliance.ms/

Momentum
Grand Rapids, MI
http://momentum-mi.com/

Excelerate Labs
Chicago, IL
http://exceleratelabs.com/

BetaSpring
Providence, RI
http://betaspring.com/

GRA
Atlanta, GA
http://www.gra.org/

Shotput Ventures
Atlanta, GA
http://www.shotputventures.com/

Innovation Depot
Birmingham, AL
http://www.innovationdepot.net/

The Idea Village
New Orleans, LA
http://ideavillage.org/

LaunchBox Digital
Durham, NC
http://www.launchboxdigital.com/

NextStart
Greenville, SC
http://www.nextstart.org/

VMASC
Suffolk, VA
http://www.vmasc.odu.edu/

JumpStart Foundry
Nashville, TN
http://jumpstartfoundry.com/

Innovation to Enterprise
Oklahoma City, OK
http://www.i2e.org/

Pipeline Entrepreneurs
Kansas City, KA
http://pipelineentrepreneurs.com/

RRV Research Corridor
Fargo, ND
http://www.theresearchcorridor.com/

NEHLA
Kona, HI
http://www.nelha.org/

Also see local funding foundations listed by state at
http://www.tgci.com/funding.shtml

BIBLIOGRAPHY

&

RECOMMENDED FURTHER READING

13th Annual NIH SBIR/STTR Conference, June 22-23, 2011, Bethesda, MD.

Aquent Creative Team. *Adobe Creative Suite 4 Digital Classroom*. Indianapolis, IN, U.S.A.: Wiley, 2009.

Bagley CE, Dauchy CE. *The Entrepreneur's Guide to Business Law*, 3rd Ed. Mason, OH, U.S.A.: Thomson West, 2007.

Berkery D. *Raising Venture Capital for the Serious Entrepreneur*. New York, NY, U.S.A.: McGraw-Hill, 2008.

Code of Federal Regulations (C.F.R.) Title 2, 2011, Government Printing Office http://www.gpoaccess.gove/cfr/index.html.

Code of Federal Regulations (C.F.R.), Title 21, 2011, Government Printing Office http://www.gpoaccess.gove/cfr/index.html.

Code of Federal Regulations (C.F.R.), Title 42, 2011, Government Printing Office http://www.gpoaccess.gove/cfr/index.html.

Code of Federal Regulations (C.F.R.), Title 45, 2011, Government Printing Office http://www.gpoaccess.gove/cfr/index.html.

Code of Federal Regulations (C.F.R.), Title 48, 2011, Government Printing Office http://www.gpoaccess.gove/cfr/index.html.

Einstein A. "I am enough of an artist to draw freely upon my imagination. Imagination is more important than knowledge." Interview by George Sylvester Viereck, "What Life Means to Einstein," *Saturday Evening Post*. Vol. 202, Oct 26, 1929.

Einstein A. "I have no special talents. I am only passionately curious." Letter to Carl Seelig, Mar 11, 1952, *Albert Einstein Archives 39-013*.

Einstein A. "It is in fact nothing short of a miracle that modern methods of instruction have not yet entirely strangled the holy curiosity of inquiry; for this delicate little plant, aside from stimulation, stands mainly in need of freedom; without this it goes to wrack and ruin without fail." Autobiographical notes, *Albert Einstein: Philosopher-Scientist*, Ed. Paul Arthur Schilpp: Library of Living Philosophers, La Salle, 1949.

Einstein A. "Only someone who is not seeking is safe from error," translated from, *"Nur wer nicht sucht, ist vor Irrtum sicher."* Letter to Gustav Bucky, Summer 1945, *Albert Einstein Archives* 37-462.

Einstein A. "Science is a wonderful thing if one does not have to earn one's living at it." Draft letter to student E. Holzapfel, March 1951, *Albert Einstein Archives 59-1013/1014*.

Eliot TS. *The Waste Land.* New York: Boni and Liveright, 1922.

Emerson RW. "Progress of Culture," *Letters and Social Aims.* Boston: James R. Osgood and Company, 1876.

Emerson RW. "Wealth," *The Conduct of Life.* London: Smith, Elder and Company, 1860.

Feynman R. "I am sure of nothing, and find myself having to say 'I don't know' very often. After all, I was born not knowing and have only had a little time to change that here and there. It is fun to find things you thought you knew, and then to discover you didn't really understand it after all." Letter to Armando Garcia J, Dec 11, 1985, in *Perfectly Reasonable Deviations from the Beaten Track: The Letters of Richard P. Feynman,"* Edited by Michelle Feynman. New York, U.S.A.: Basic Books, 2006. (Used with permission of The Perseus Books Group.)

Friedman Y. *Building Biotechnology.* Washington DC, U.S.A.: Logos Press, 2008.

Frost R. "The Road Not Taken," *Mountain Interval.* New York: Henry Holt and Company, 1916.

Kaplan AV, Baim DS, Smith JJ, Feigal DA, Simons M, Jefferys D, Fogarty TJ, Kuntz RE, Leon MB. "Medical device development: from prototype to regulatory approval." *Circulation*. 109(25):3068-72, 2004.

Lo J, Pressman D. *How to Make Patent Drawings*, 5th Ed. U.S.A.: NOLO, 2007.

Pasteur L. "Fortune favors the prepared mind," translated from, "*Dans les champs de l'observation le hazard ne favorise que les esprits prepares.*" University of Lille Lecture, Dec 7, 1854.

Pressman D. *Patent It Yourself: Your Step-by-Step Guide to Filing at the U.S. Patent Office*, 14th Ed. U.S.A.: NOLO, 2009.

Preston SL. *Angel Financing for Entrepreneurs: Early Stage Funding for Long-Term Success*. San Francisco, CA, U.S.A.: Jossey-Bass, 2007.

Silbiger S. *The Ten Day MBA*, 3rd Ed. New York, U.S.A.: HarperCollins Publishers, 2005.

Tennyson A. "Ulysses," *Poems*. London: Edward Moxon, 1842.

Thoreau HD. *Walden; or, Life in the Woods*. Boston: Ticknor and Fields, 1854. (The irony of quoting Thoreau in a business book is not lost on the author, my sincerest apologies.)

Wilde O. *Lady Windermere's Fan*. London: Elkin Matthews and John Lane, 1893.

INDEX

169

ABOUT THE AUTHOR

Richard J. McMurtrey is a physician and scientist who has worked in a wide variety of fields, including neuroscience, biochemistry, and biomedical engineering, and he has received many awards, grants, and honors for his research work. He also trained in neurosurgery and critical care, and is the founder of Skyentia Technologies, which seeks to develop biomolecular neural interfaces. In his spare time he enjoys exploring the outdoors, collecting books, and playing classical piano.

17371681R00097

Made in the USA
Lexington, KY
06 September 2012